the GREEN SEA *of* HEAVEN

Fifty ghazals *from the Díwán of Ḥáfiẓ*

Translated by ELIZABETH T. GRAY, JR.
With an Introduction by Daryush Shayegan

WHITE CLOUD PRESS
ASHLAND, OREGON

White Cloud Press, P. O. Box 3400, Ashland, Oregon 97520.

99 98 97 96 5 4 3 2 1

Cover Design by Dan Cook
Cover Illustration by Shohreh Shakib
Printed in the United States of America

LIBRARY OF CONGRESS CATALOGING IN PUBLICATION DATA

Ḥáfiẓ, 14th cent.
[Díván. English & Persian. Selections]
The green sea of heaven : fifty ghazals from the Díwán of Ḥáfiẓ / translated by Elizabeth T. Gray ; with a foreword by Daryush Shayegan
p. cm.
Includes bibliographical references.
ISBN 1-883991-06-4 : $14.95
1. Ḥáfiẓ, 14th cent.--Translations into English.
I. Gray, Elizabeth T., 1952- . II. Title
PK6465.Z32G73 1994 94-19633 CIP
891'.5511--dc20

Early drafts of these translations appeared in *Antaeus* (1979), *The Falcon* (1979), *The Agni* (1979), and *Ploughshares* (1985).

the GREEN SEA *of* HEAVEN

THE WHITE CLOUD PRESS
LIBRARY OF PERSIA:
TEXTS AND CONTEXTS IN PERSIAN RELIGIONS AND SPIRITUALITY

BOOKS IN THE SERIES:
Creation and the Timeless Order of Things:
Essays in Islamic Mystical Philosophy
by Toshihiko Izutsu

The Green Sea of Heaven:
Fifty ghazals from the Díwán of Ḥáfiẓ
Translated by Elizabeth T. Gray, Jr.

سخن اندر دهان دوست گوهر
ولیکن گفتهٔ حافظ از آن بـــه

In the mouth of the beloved speech is a jewel.
However, the verse of Ḥáfiẓ is better than that.

Contents

For Jim and Jeanne

Acknowledgments

Ultimately the translator is responsible for the choices he or she makes, for what is caught and what is missed. While acknowledging that responsibility I must be clear that these translations reflect learnings over many years from many people.

I have been blessed with advice, instruction, and encouragement from an array of extraordinary scholars, translators, and poets. In the early seventies at Harvard University I learned Persian from Wheeler Thackston, first encountered Ḥáfiẓ under the encouraging eye of Hossein Ziai, and had the opportunity to study under, and travel briefly in North India with, Professor Annemarie Schimmel. Waris Kirmani, at the University of Aligarh, India, and Farhang Jahanpour and Muhammad Qa'emi at the University of Isfahan, Iran, both helped me work through a number of ghazals. Bruce Lawrence, at Duke University, and Jim Morris, at the Imperial Iranian Academy of Philosophy, the Institute for Ismaili Studies in Paris, and Oberlin College, reviewed early drafts and offered encouragement. In 1989 Michael Sells, at Haverford, urged me to return to the manuscript and revise it for publication and offered insightful suggestions. During the past year Iraj Anvar, at New York University, has collaborated with me on revising the poems and notes. The gentle insistence and suggestions of Steven Scholl at White Cloud Press have been invaluable. Their views, their learning, their experience, and their own personal responses to Ḥáfiẓ have informed my own understanding of his work, and thus the shape of these translations. I am grateful for their time, their encouragement, their humor, and their skepticism.

Elizabeth Bishop, by her example as a translator and her powerful insistence that I focus meticulously on what Ḥáfiẓ actually *said,* was helpful in curbing excesses that arose from early enthusiasm combined with a partial understanding of the Persian. Robert Lowell's terse and scathing dismissal of some early drafts was personally devastating and saved me years of work. Robert Fitzgerald's encouragement, and his stubborn insistence on the value of the work, were helpful when I was working with him and have sustained me since his death. Listening to him share at great length his dilemma with a passage of Virgil was one of the most illuminating experiences I have ever had. His long, tangible, complicated, and intimate relationships with Homer and Virgil, and his attention to scholarship as well as poetry, continue to be a source of inspiration. To some degree, these translations remain an offering to him.

E.T.G., Jr.
October 1994
New York City

Translator's Introduction

Khwája Shams ud-Dín Muḥammad Ḥáfiẓ-i Shírází (d. 1389) is acknowledged to be the unrivalled master of the classical Persian *ghazal*, a brief and strict lyric form. Throughout the Persian-speaking world one hears his verses recited or sung in the bazaar, on the radio, and at spiritual gatherings. His *Díwán*, or collected works, is held in such high esteem that, like the Qur'án, it is used for divination and augury. Nevertheless, about Ḥáfiẓ's life we have legends but few facts. We do not even have an authentic text of his *Díwán*.

Ḥáfiẓ and His Historical Context

The extant sources of biographical information—a preface to an early edition of his work, anecdotes and biographical sketches, references by other writers, the poems themselves—strengthen some of the legends and bring others into question, but are not ultimately reliable. What we have are facts about his life that seem consistent among the sources, and we know that the era in which he lived was one of both political chaos and extraordinary literary and artistic achievement. We know that he lived in one of the most beautiful cities in the world.

Ḥáfiẓ was born in Isfahan, in what is now central Iran, somewhere between 1317 and 1325. His father, Bahá' ud-Dín, was a merchant, and moved his family south from Isfahan to the city of Shiraz when Ḥáfiẓ was a young boy.[1] Shiraz lies along the banks of the Ruknabad river, in the province of Fars, nestled in a circle of mountains and surrounded by vineyards. In Ḥáfiẓ's day it was a flourishing center of Islamic civilization, and he developed a deep and lifelong affection for the city. Then, as now, it was famous for its beauty, its wines, and its exquisite gardens.

Ḥáfiẓ's father died when Ḥáfiẓ was still a child, leaving the family in difficult circumstances. Nevertheless, Ḥáfiẓ seems to have acquired a thorough and comprehensive classical education. He was fluent in the Persian and Arabic languages and traditions, and educated in the quranic sciences. His pen name, Ḥáfiẓ ("the preserver," "the guardian"), implies that he could recite the entire Qur'án from memory. He is said to have worked as a baker's apprentice and a copyist until he found adequate patronage for his poetry, and is said to have taught in one of Shiraz's theological schools later in his life.

Ḥáfiẓ was born in the last days of the Íl-Khánid empire established by Hülegü Khán. A grandson of Chingiz Khán, Hülegü was best known for his sack of Baghdad, the capital of the far reaching 'Abbasid empire, in 1258. During Ḥáfiẓ's childhood and adolescence the Íl-Khánid empire disintegrated into small rival states and factions. Rebellion, civil war, and intradynastic treachery were common, and cities changed hands many times. A brief discussion of the squabbling dynasties that existed in southern Iran during Ḥáfiẓ's lifetime will give the modern reader a sense for the context in which Ḥáfiẓ wrote, and perhaps a better understanding of the poet and his work. Although of little importance in the grand scheme of Islamic history, these minor rulers were the patrons upon whose favor Ḥáfiẓ depended for his life and livelihood.

While Ḥáfiẓ was in his teens Sháh Abú Isḥáq of the Injú dynasty consolidated power in Fars after a seven-year struggle with his three brothers. Abú Isḥáq was a tolerant ruler, easy-going and artistically inclined, and brought stability to the region. We know that Ḥáfiẓ's literary career began to flourish during Abú Isḥáq's twelve-year reign because several of his poems mention patrons who served as viziers at Abú Isḥáq's court.[2] In 1353 Abú Isḥáq was overthrown and eventually executed by Sháh Mubariz ud-Dín Muḥammad, founder of the Muẓaffarid dynasty based in Yazd. In contrast to Abú Isḥáq, Mubariz was a strictly orthodox Muslim, and both courtly delights and the taverns of Shiraz suffered during the five years of his puritanical rule. Despite the artistic chill, and perhaps demonstrating a high degree of skill in political adaptation, Ḥáfiẓ continued to write at court, perhaps under the patronage of Mubariz's Chief Minister.[3] Returning from a successful campaign against Isfahan and Tabriz in 1358, Mubariz was deposed, blinded, and thrown in prison by his two sons, who divided their father's kingdom between them. Quṭb ud-Dín Maḥmúd claimed Isfahan, and Jalál ud-Dín Sháh Shujá‘ began his long reign in Shiraz, which, although troubled, saw the expansion of Sháh Shujá‘'s dominion over much of the old Íl-Khánid empire.

Sháh Shujá‘ was not only a consistent patron of the arts and of learning, but a poet in his own right, both in Persian and Arabic. It was during his 27-year reign that Ḥáfiẓ flourished, and wrote the poetry that became famous throughout the Islamic world. Apparently the relationship between Ḥáfiẓ and his ruler/patron was not always smooth. One story suggests that Ḥáfiẓ fell out of favor for mocking both Sháh Shujá‘'s panegyrist[4] and those less skilled in the crafting of verse (presumably including Sháh Shujá‘). During this time he is said to have spent one or two years in Isfahan and Yazd, but we have no certain evidence of this. Aside from this interlude of disfavor, and despite lucrative offers of patronage from courts as far away as Baghdad and India, Ḥáfiẓ could never bring himself to leave Shiraz.

By 1380, when Ḥáfiẓ was in his sixties, Timur Lang (known to Occidentals as "Tamerlane") had consolidated power in Central Asia north of the Oxus river, and turned his attention to the the territories of the old Íl-Khánid empire. In 1380 his assaults on the provinces of Khurasan, Sistan, and Mazandaran laid waste to the countryside and razed any town that tried to defend itself. As an instrument of war his use of terror was meticulous and persuasive: the story of 2,000 defenders of a town in Sistan who were built into a wall while still alive traveled quickly, and served as a vivid reminder of the price of resistance. In 1382 Timur again came south into Persia, but a negotiated truce between Timur and Sháh Shujá‘ ensured that the Muẓaffarid possessions were spared the horrors visited on neighboring provinces.

In 1387 the Muẓaffarids were not so lucky. Sháh Shujá‘ had been succeeded by his son, Zayn ul-‘Ábidín, who declined to offer obeisance to Timur in person. Aggravated by this display of disrespect Timur marched against Fars, and upon arriving in Isfahan demanded a hefty financial contribution from its inhabitants. The rebuke tendered by the Isfahanis included the killing of several of Timur's tax collectors. In response Timur looted the city and massacred its entire population. He had a tall minaret of 70,000 skulls built as a grim memorial, and proceeded south toward Shiraz. Zayn ul-‘Ábidín fled to Shushtar, where he was promptly blinded and imprisoned by his cousin. Timur entered Shiraz without bloodshed.

The legendary meeting between Timur and Ḥáfiẓ is said to have taken place during Timur's soujourn in Shiraz. Timur is said to have called Ḥáfiẓ into his presence to scold him for the following *bayt*:

> If that Turk of Shiraz would take my heart in his hand, I would give for his Hindu [i.e. black] mole both Bukhárá and Samarqand.

Timur pointed out that he had conquered and plundered much of the world in order to build and beautify Bukhara and Samarqand, his native cities and seat of government. He was incensed that Ḥáfiẓ could suggest trading both for the affection of a young, lithe, Turkish slave with a beauty mark. Ḥáfiẓ, with a deep bow, is said to have replied, "Sir, it is because of such prodigality that I have fallen into poverty and hard times." Timur was apparently charmed, and ordered that Ḥáfiẓ be rewarded instead of imprisoned.

Between 1387 and 1392 various Muẓaffarid brothers and cousins fought for control of Shiraz, Yazd, Kirman, and other cities in Fars. In 1392 Timur ended the family dispute by taking Shiraz and executing the remaining dynastic contenders, with the exception of the blind Zayn ul-'Ábidín, whom he took with him to Samarqand. Timur's pursuit of conquest and terror continued (he executed 100,000 people in Delhi in 1398). Upon his death in 1405 he was succeeded by his son, Sháh Rukh, who had difficulty in holding together the empire his father had created.

Ḥáfiẓ did not live to see the demise of the Muẓaffarids. He died in 1389 or 1390, and was buried in the Musalla Gardens, which lie gracefully along the banks of the Ruknabad river in the city he loved so well. As he predicted in several of his *ghazals*, his tomb and its surrounding gardens became a place of pilgrimage, and remain so to this day.

LITERATURE AT COURT

To understand the role of the poet at court in the fourteenth century we must examine courtly tradition in Persia before the advent of Islam.[5] Pre-Islamic Persia was primarily an urban society governed by kings who kept their ceremonial distance from the populace and were considered almost, if not actually, divine. Court life was elaborate and elegant, and the formal ranks of the nobility placed great emphasis on courtly manners and appropriate behavior. The king's retinue included musicians, dancers, singers, and other entertainers. Of these, the poet's place was considered highly prestigious. Poets and their patrons had a special relationship with one another: the patron provided security, support, and privilege; the poet served as entertainer, panegyrist, and, as appropriate, intimate counsellor. Most of this courtly tradition was incorporated by Islamic and Arab rulers, and did not change dramatically during the Mongol era.

In the fourteenth century rulers and their ministers were the primary patrons of the arts, including poetry, and the arts flourished during these turbulent times. Poetry was composed for the patron and his retinue, who were usually well-educated in the Persian and Arabic language and literary traditons. Poetry was recited orally, or sung, in this very public context, as entertainment or diversion, as an offering for a specific occasion, as an entry in a poetic competition, or as a general or specific statement on a topic. Poets used a variety of poetic forms, of which the *ghazal* was one.

THE *GHAZAL*

FORMAL REQUIREMENTS

Ḥáfiẓ's *Díwán* consists almost entirely of *ghazals*, and he so perfected this formidable verse form that none of his many successors has ever matched his depth, elegance, and precision. The classical Persian *ghazal* has between five and twelve lines (*bayts*), each of which is divided into two hemistitches (*miṣra'*). In the opening *bayts* (the *maṭla'*), each *miṣra'* ends in an identical rhyme, and this monorhyme is repeated at the end of each *bayt* for the remainder of the poem. Often the rhyme includes one or more words (*radíf*), not simply the final syllable.

Although Persian is an accentual, Indo-European language, the meters used in Persian verse are quantitative, and were adopted from classical Arabic prosody. The first *miṣra'* sets the meter to which all other *miṣra'* conform, although on occasion the poet may substitute two short syllables for one long syllable. Depending on the meter, a *bayts* may have between twenty-four and thirty-two syllables. The rhythmical pattern and rhyme scheme can be seen in the following diagram of a *ghazal* in a typical meter (*Ramal sálim makhbún maḥdhúf*). The reader needs to bear in mind that Persian is read from right to left.

A -- --oo --oo --o-	A -- --oo --oo --o-
A -- --oo --oo --o-	B -- --oo --oo --o-
A -- --oo --oo --o-	C -- --oo --oo --o-
A -- --oo --oo --o-	D -- --oo --oo --o-
A -- --oo --oo --o-	E -- --oo --oo --o-

F -- --oo --oo --o-
A -- --oo --oo --o-

As a rule, the last *bayt* (*maqṭa'*) contains the poet's name or pen name (*takhallus*). While the complex and rigid requirements of the *ghazal* form defeated many less talented poets, it forced others, like Ḥáfiẓ, to write verse of compressed and brilliant intensity.

ORIGINS AND EVOLUTION

While the term *ghazal* can be used in a general way to mean a genre of lyric poetry concerned primarily with love, in its more restricted sense it means the formal, classical Persian lyric perfected in the thirteenth and fourteenth centuries. From uncertain origins, it has evolved differently in the Arabic, Persian, Ottoman, and Urdu literary traditions.[6]

Some believe that the classical Persian *ghazal* evolved from the *nasíb*, the brief and often erotic prologue to the Arabic *qaṣída*, a longer ode with a *ghazal*-like rhyme scheme composed on panegyric, didactic, elegiac, or religious subjects.[7] Others believe the *ghazal* developed from early Iranian folk poetry, about which we know nothing. Others believe it to be a blending of indigenous Persian lyric with the more formal structures and themes of earlier Arabic poetry.

By the tenth century the traditional themes explored by early *ghazal* composers had hardened into literary convention. Thereafter, in addition to the rhetorical figures and embellishments required of all good Persian poetry, the conservative taste of the Persian courts demanded that poets continue to improvise on the themes of love, longing, wine, intoxication, separation and sorrow, roses, nightingales, deserts, and departing caravans. Excellence lay not in creating a new or unique image, but in using the familiar images and conventions in innovative ways.

In the twelfth and thirteenth centuries the *ghazal* underwent a decisive alteration. What had been a courtly love lyric concerned with actual wine and physical beauty became, in the hands of great Sufi writers like

Faríd ud-Dín 'Aṭṭár (1142-1220) and Jalál ud-Dín Rúmí (1207-1273), both a vehicle to describe the mystic's loving relationship with God and also a means of veiling from theological and political conservatives the Sufi belief in the possibility of an intutive, personal union of God and man.[8] This infusion of mysticism enriched the *ghazal* and opened the traditional themes to new dimensions of interpretation. The symbols brought to the form by Sufi writers became, in their turn, literary conventions.

The *ghazal* reached its high level of formal development with the work of Muṣlih ud-Dín Sa'dí (1256-1292), also of Shiraz, author of the famous *Gulistán.* His *ghazals* were beautifully composed around a single theme, usually of a more moralistic than spiritual nature. Fifty years later Ḥáfiẓ, in command of the *ghazal*'s traditional imagery and themes and at home with its intricate formal requirements, blended eroticism, mysticism, and panegyric into verse of unsurpassed beauty.

CONVENTIONS AND IMAGERY

CONVENTIONS

These *ghazals* are often puzzling to the "Westerner" who approaches them for the first time. The same images reappear in poem after poem after poem after poem. The poems do not seem to go anywhere: there is no opening, no action, no ultimate resolution or answer. Sometimes the lines seem unrelated to one another. And everything seems ambiguous: is the poet talking to the one he loves? Or is he reproaching a patron? Or is this a nugget of wisdom aimed at the disciple who seeks union with God? If the poet is talking to or about his beloved, is the beloved a man or a woman? Is it actually the poet talking? And isn't drinking alcohol a violation of Islamic law?

At first glance, and in comparison with other classical Persian literary forms (the panegyric *qaṣída,* the romance, the narrative *mathnawí,* the witty *rubá'í*), the *ghazal* seems to be a personal or even confessional poem. The poet seems to sharing his personal feelings. With time it becomes clear that this is not the case. The poet is using an array of personae and images to speak of love in a way that expresses an ideal, and does so within a fiction. The troubador poets in medieval Europe crafted their songs in a similar way.

The poet who declares his identity in the closing *bayt* of the *ghazal*, the voice speaking throughout the *ghazal*, is a persona. It is the "I" of an "I-Thou" relationship, and the "I" speaks of his searing love for the perpetually unreachable "Thou." The "I" and "Thou" may be lover and beloved, poet and patron, mystic and God, or the poet may intend a *bayt* or *ghazal* to suggest all of these relationships. However it is framed, the *ghazal* deals with unconditional love and devotion, the anguish of separation and longing, the ecstasy of union, the creation of obligations, and the honoring of promises.

The ambiguities that surround the speaker and the object of his love stem from a variety of sources. The politics of court and Islamic prohibitions against extramarital relationships forced the poet to veil the identity of his beloved. Refined tact and diplomacy were important in addressing powerful and perhaps capricious patrons whose power over one's life and livelihood was absolute. References to things considered heretical by Islam could not be discussed too explicitly.

In addition, poets took advantage of the fact that Persian pronouns do not indicate gender. It is usually impossible to tell whether the Beloved is male or female or divine. Ḥáfiẓ exploited these ambiguities, powerfully and artfully, to suggest different types of "I-Thou" relationships and to create resonances between them.[9] It is why "every listener seems to find in it an answer to his question, every reader thinks he is discovering an allusion to his desire."[10]

IMAGERY

Ḥáfiẓ could draw upon, and was constrained by, the rich array of images and analogies that had been used and developed in the preceding centuries. To the well-educated courtly listener each image held, embedded within it, a host of associations and recollections. Delighting an audience demanded verse act like a prism, bringing different light from new angles to a rich and familiar image. Ḥáfiẓ used imagery from many sources: stories and sayings from the Islamic tradition, from pre-Islamic Persian epics, Sufi literature, astronomy, astrology, alchemy, and the flora and fauna of Shiraz's gardens. To offer here a lengthy explanation and analysis of the various elements that make up the *ghazal*'s canon of imagery would not be fruitful. Some are discussed in Daryush Shayegan's Introduction, others in the footnotes to the individual *ghazals*.[11] Nevertheless, a brief sketch of the cast of characters and primary images will be helpful to the reader encountering these poems for the first time.

There is the Beloved, who has the tall and swaying stature of the cypress, and the radiant, pure, and perfect face of the moon. The Lover seeks union with the Beloved, to give up his soul to the Beloved, to become lost or annihilated in the Beloved as the moth is consumed by the flame to which it is attracted. The Beloved is the source and incarnation of love and beauty, the ultimately beautiful rose unfolding in the garden, and the Lover, pining in separation or loss, begs the dawn wind or the hoopoe to act as a messenger or go-between, to bring news of the Beloved, to carry a message or plaint to him (or her).

The true Lover understands the ecstasy and the pain of loving, for him it is both his elixir and his daily bread. He is the one for whom Love is the sole spiritual imperative, the ultimate intoxicant, the only law that governs an enlightened soul. Lovers are the disciples of Beauty, disciples of the Beloved, disciples of Love. They take up the path of Love and pass through its waystations under the guidance of a Master, a wise elder (the *pír*). The *rends*[12] are Lovers: they adhere only to Love's law, and to the uninitiated their behavior seems dissolute and blasphemous.

Arrayed in opposition to the Lover are the false Lovers and the enforcers of orthodoxy. The orthodox scholars and judges preach and enforce the Islamic law, or *sharí'a.* They condemn intoxication, they demand penitence, they insist on correct behavior. Ḥáfiẓ mocks them because in their blind adherence to the letter of Islamic law they miss God and His message completely. Their own corrupt behavior is at variance with their preachings and prohibitions. They are blind to what matters.[13]

There is also the rival, the impostor or pretender, the *mudda'í,* who claims to understand Love, who claims intimacy with the Beloved. The impostor's words are empty of wisdom, he is not an intimate of the secrets. Nevertheless, he babbles on about love, offering his audience unenlightened verse.

A word on taverns, wine, winemasters, cupbearers, and Zoroastrians is in order. Islam's prohibition against drinking alcohol meant that within the Islamic world the making and serving of wine fell to Zoroastrians and Christians and others. Nevertheless, in Ḥáfiẓ's *ghazals* the "tavern of the Magi" usually suggests an esoteric sanctuary or gathering, an assembly of believers, which exists beyond the borders of orthodox Islam.[14] It was wise to veil one's speech when discussing such things.

Wine drinking parties were a regular and elaborate fixture of courtly life.[15] At these gatherings wine was served by young Turkic slaves, imported from northern Iran and Central Asia as children. They were taught weaponry and riding, to sing and to serve wine. They were thought most beautiful just at the moment that they entered puberty, when the first traces of facial hair became visible. These cupbearers were the object of poetic and physical love. While in Western literature we are unaccustomed, and uncomfortable, with homoerotic love, the reader should understand that by convention the Beloved is male.[16]

UNITY: THE ONGOING DEBATE

To the reader accustomed to Western literature the *ghazal* is puzzling and perhaps frustrating: there is no plot, no narrative, no movement toward a climax or resolution in the sense that Westerners understand dramatic development. Indeed, depending on the edition, Ḥáfiẓ's *bayts* in a specific *ghazal* may appear in a different sequences, rarely affecting the *ghazal*'s power as a poem.

Apparently Sháh Shujá' was the first person to raise the question of whether, or in what manner, there is "unity" in Ḥáfiẓ's *ghazals.* Ḥáfiẓ supposedly answered to the effect that most people seemed to like his poems, and that in fact while other poets had trouble finding an audience beyond their own city gates, Ḥáfiẓ's poems were read throughout the Islamic world.[17] While acknowledging the truth of Ḥáfiẓ's response, others continue to debate Sháh Shujá''s question. Opinions as to whether the *ghazals* have "unity", and if so, in what way, have varied with the fashions of literary critcism.[18]

Some Western critics decided that atomism was the defining principle: there was no unifying element, each *bayt* was like a perfect, separate pearl. The *ghazal* was simply a series of pearls on a string of a certain length, "orient pearls at random strung."[19] Other readers have felt a sense of completeness, of "unity," in a Ḥáfiẓean *ghazal,* and have tried in different ways to describe its source. Some find it to be similar to the pattern in a carpet or tapestry: variations of shape and color that repeat and connect to form a whole. Others describe it as a crystal, each facet illuminating a different aspect of one or several themes. Some have described the *ghazal* as polyphonic or contrapuntal, having two or three themes that weave together, and recur in different forms, in different registers. Some have likened the *ghazal* to the surface of a pool: from two or three themes dropped like pebbles come concentric rings of images that expand, intersect, and create patterns of resonance. Suffice it to say that *ghazals* are not like any other "Western" lyric. For centuries people have been deeply moved by these poems, and I would urge the reader approaching these *ghazals* for the first time to question his or her own embedded literary assumptions and to brandish lightly, at the outset, the templates of Western literary criticism.

TEXTUAL PROBLEMS

We have no established text of Ḥáfiẓ's *Díwán*, and it seems that Ḥáfiẓ did not compile one during his lifetime.[20] The editions that proliferated throughout the Islamic world after his death attest to the quality and fame of his work, but as they grew in number the texts themselves became more corrupt. Even if Ḥáfiẓ had circulated different versions of specific *ghazals*, or had revised and edited earlier *ghazals* as he went along, it would not explain the alterations and expanded editions. Copyists the world over are likely to misread or miscopy manuscripts, and might "improve" a *bayt* by substituting a "better" word, but it seems that lines in similar meters by other authors, or whole *ghazals*, may have been added to "enhance" the edition. Lesser writers may have sought to ensure that their work would live forever by inserting a *ghazal* of their own among those of Ḥáfiẓ.

Since the early sixteenth century efforts have been made to define an authentic *Díwán*. The preface to an early edition by Ḥáfiẓ's "friend" Gulandam suggests that it is a first edition, but that assumption has not been tested. Qazvíní's and Ghání's 1941 critical edition was based on the oldest manuscripts available at the time, and in their judgment none of these four manuscripts upon which they relied was related to the others. Since 1941 more than fourteen manuscripts have come to light that appear to pre-date the ones used by Qazvíní and Ghání, but they have not been extensively studied in relation to one another. More work needs to be done, and may or may not result in an authentic text.

Khánlari's edition was used for these translations, and the editions by Qazvíní and Ghání, by Ahmad and Ná'íní, and by Anjaví were consulted.

In addition, I have drawn extensively on the commentaries by Khurram Sháhí, Rajá'í, and Súdí, and consulted teachers, scholars, and advisors in the U.S., Iran, and India, as well as previous translations of Ḥáfiẓ's work.

NOTES

Please refer to the bibliography for complete information on sources cited.

1. Sources differ on the date of his birth. Some also say that it was Ḥáfiẓ's grandfather, rather than his father, who moved to Shiraz from Isfahan. Some give his father's name as Kamál ul-Dín. Edward G. Browne's *Literary History of Persia*, Volume III, gives an extensive and colorful history of both Ḥáfiẓ's life and the chaotic times in which he lived.

2. See, for example, Ghazal 5, where Qavám ud-Dín Ḥasan is mentioned, and related notes.

3. Burhán ud-Dín Fatḥ Alláh was supposedly Mubariz's Chief Minister.

4. 'Imád ud-Dín Faqíh was Sháh Shujá''s official panegyrist.

5. Julie Scott Meisami's *Medieval Persian Court Poetry* discusses at length courtly traditions, the relationship between poet and patron, and the various types of poetry that flourished in that milieu (panegyric odes, romances, and *ghazals*).

6. Alessandro Bausani's article on "The Ghazal" and its evolution can be found in the *Encyclopedia of Islam (New Edition)*, Vol. III, and readers seeking more extensive information are advised to begin with this source.

7. Jan Rypka and others, *History of Iranian Literature*, p. 94. For a thorough introduction to, and translations of, the Arabic *qaṣída*, see Michael Sells's *Desert Tracings*.

8. Rypka, p. 232.

9. While the Persian pronouns' ambiguity of gender (and its lack of distinction between upper and lower case letters) enhances the allusiveness available to the poet, the English translator is forced on some occasions to choose between the masculine, the feminine, and the Divine. Throughout these translations I have elected to use lowercase letters unless it is clear that Ḥáfiẓ is referring to God, and have tried vigilantly to avoid having to make a choice of gender. Nevertheless, some *ghazals* speak of a masculine beloved (the standard assumption in classical Persian poetry), and some of a feminine beloved (the standard assumption in English poetry). Within *ghazals* I have tried to remain consistent. The reader should continually remember that the original Persian is not so constrained.

10. See Daryush Shayegan's Introduction, p. 16

11. The most comprehensive description and analysis of imagery within the Persian poetic tradition in English is Annemarie Schimmel's *A Two-Colored Brocade.* It includes examples drawn from a range of Islamic literatures.

12. See Shayegan, Introduction, pp. 28ff.

13. See, for example, Ḥáfiẓ's view of these pillars of orthodoxy in Ghazal 31; and also Shayegan's discussion of Ḥáfiẓ's subversive audacity, his continuing role as "one of the greatest protesters in history," Introduction, pp. 32-34.

14. See Shayegan, Introduction, pp. 24-25.

15. See "The Theme of Wine Drinking and the Concept of he Beloved in Early Persian Poetry", by Ehsan Yarshater.

16. See above, note 9.

17. Hillman, *Unity in the Ghazals of Ḥáfiẓ.*

18. Some of the primary contributors to this discussion have been Arberry, Rehder, Wickens, Hillman, Boyce, Meisami, and Schimmel. The reader who wishes to explore this topic further, or to see how differing theories are applied to specific *ghazals*, should begin with these authors.

19. Sir William Jones, "A Persian Song", 1771, in A. J. Arberry's, "Ḥáfiẓ and his English Translators".

20. Rehder's "The Text of Ḥáfiẓ" and "New Material for the Text of Ḥáfiẓ" offer a comprehensive discussion of the *Díwán*'s history, and the existing textual problems.

The Visionary Topography of Ḥáfiẓ*

by Daryush Shayegan

Khwája Shams ud-Dín Muḥammad Ḥáfiẓ-i Shírází, the Persian poet of the fourteenth century, is one of the greatest mystics and lyrical poets of all time. The Iranian tradition has designated him the *lisán-al-ghayb*, "the tongue of the Invisible" and *tarjumán al-asrár*, "the interpreter of the mysteries." And this for good reason, for of all the poets who have written in Persian—and there are very many of them—he has enjoyed the most privileged position, being, as it were, the intimate interlocutor of every heart in distress, of every soul that is seized by mystical exaltation. It is no accident therefore that Persians often consult his *Díwán*, in the same way that the Chinese consult the *I Ching*.

Being the interpreter of the mysteries, Ḥáfiẓ is also an undisputed master of spiritual hermeneutic (*ta'wíl*); I would even say that his vision is fashioned of the *ta'wíl*, as the poet not only searches into the unfathomable mysteries which open up thanks to the divine theophanies, but he is himself the locus where these same theophanies unveil themselves. This vision is reflected as much in the structure of his *ghazals* as in the almost magical perfection of his word, and in the sovereign art with which he maintains complete and undisputed mastery over all the resources and nuances of the Persian language; this vision is such that with him the art

* "The Visionary Topography of Ḥáfiẓ" was delivered at the 1980 session of l'Université Saint Jean de Jérusalem and published in Cahier No. 7, *L'Hermeneutique Permanente* (Paris: Berg International). Adapted from the translation from the French by Lana and Peter Russell for the journal *Temenos.*

of the mystical lyric reaches an apotheosis that has never been surpassed: he marks both the supreme flowering and the uttermost limit of his art.

All the millennary genius of Persian art: the judicious equilibrium between form and content, the economy of means, the striking concision of paradoxical ideas, the affective and polyvalent tonalities of verbal magic amplifying itself on several registers, the polymorphic correspondences of symbols, the bewitching aesthetic of the Eternal Feminine scattered like so many alluring images in the world's mirrors, condense miraculously in his art. This is why Ḥáfiẓ is not simply a great Persian poet, he is the 'miracle' of Persian literature; it is in him that the millennary sap of a culture is crystallized, which, grafting the prophetic tradition of the Muhammadan Revelation on to the ancient spirit of Iran, made a synthesis so full, so profound, that it became, as it were, the *humanitas* of all Islam, oriental and Iranian.

Every Persian has a private bond with Ḥáfiẓ. It matters little whether he is learned, mystic, unlettered, or *rend* (inspired libertine), as Ḥáfiẓ called himself. Every Persian finds in him a part of himself, discovers in him an unexplored niche in his own memory, a fragrant recollection from the interior garden of which he is the unique guardian. It is because of this communion that the poet's tomb is a place of pilgrimage for all Persians. Everyone goes there to seek be it but a particle of his presence: humble people from the bazaar, minor officials, intellectuals, poets, ragged beggars, all go there to collect themselves and to receive the poet's message in the silence of their heart.

How is it that Iran's most esoteric poet should also be the most popular? How do we reconcile this symbolic language with a popularity which makes the poet intimate Friend in every household? This popularity does not owe so much to the clarity of his language as to the occult correspondence which it awakens in every heart that hearkens to his call: every listener seems to find in it an answer to his question, every reader thinks he is discovering an allusion to his desire, every man finds in him a sympathetic interlocutor capable of understanding his secret, and of harmonizing it with the modulations of his song. For example, love assumes different forms according to whether it is envisaged on one level or another. It will be passionate and earthly love for some, and a profound nostalgia in quest of their original soil for others; and it will be the divine Beloved for all those who, opening themselves to what lies behind the veil of symbols, attain to a level of first events. Hence this 'connivance' of the poet with all his readers, whatever register and level they belong to.

Thus, the understanding of his hearers varies according to their knowledge, their sensibility, but each receives his or her due and no one goes away empty. With the reading of Ḥáfiẓ, as with the Qur'án, the less one comprehends intellectually, the more one receives spiritually. By the association of shaded tonalities endlessly reverberating on the keyboard of the senses, transmuting correspondences into synchronic states amplified more and more, this poetry penetrates the heart, creating a juxtaposition of states of the soul, by which the receptive soul and the symbolic tenor of the poem harmonize in the coincidence of the moment, so that this synchronicity of symbol and soul becomes the mystical configuration of a precise state.

This is also due to the particular structure of the *ghazal* itself. The reader has the impression that the poet has an eye "with multiple facets;" the world no longer unfolds itself in a simultaneous blossoming. Each distich is a complete whole, a world; within the *ghazal* one distich is not joined chronologically to the next, but is synchronically consubstantial with it. It is like a world within a larger world, which forms an integral part of the *Díwán,* as this latter forms an integral part of the cosmic vision of the poet. So, from one distich to the next, the same tonalities are amplified on extended registers, calling forth magical correspondences at every level.

The source of the energy of the poetic vision is the eye of the poet's heart, which is at once both the point of origin of all the soul's vibrations, and the center which "spatializes" the space of the vision. This synchronic coincidence of planes of vision is the beginning of the soul's dialectic movement, since the limitations of the vision are made good by a continual flow back and forth between the heart of the poet and the primeval source from which he draws his inspiration. In other words, a perpetual oscillation between self-revelation of the Divine in its self-concealment, and the concealment of the Divine in its self-revelation; between a Beauty that attracts as it repels and a Majesty that repels as it attracts. Why is the heart the starting point of this movement? Because, as Ḥáfiẓ says as he addresses the Beloved:

> Thou hast set the Treasure of Love in our ravaged heart,
> Thou has thrown the shadow of fortune over the ruined corner.

Here we encounter three essential symbols of the dialectic of love in the work of Ḥáfiẓ: that is to say, the dispenser of the Treasure of Love, Love itself, and the ravaged heart. This Treasure, the poet adds, is also a profound sorrow (*gham*), a poignant nostalgia:

> The Lord of pre-eternity (*sulṭán-i azal*) offers us the Treasure of Sorrow (*ganj-i gham-i ʻishq*)
> That we may descend into this ravaged dwelling (*manzil-i wiráneh*)

Let us look at the connotations of the symbolism of the heart in speculative gnosis.

The heart, says the Islamic mystic, is the Throne of Mercy, and Shaykh Muḥammad Láhíjí, who wrote the famous commentary on Maḥmúd Shabestarí's *Rose Garden of Mystery* (*Gulshan-i Ráz*), adds, "just as in the outside world, the Throne is the epiphany of the name of Mercy, likewise in the interior world it is the heart (*qalb*) that is its epiphany. At every breath of the Merciful One, God manifests himself in a new theophany in the heart of the believer." The heart of man is always in motion (the world *qalb* in Arabic means both "heart" and "revolution" in the sense of inversion); a motion that manifests itself in terms of renewal and resurrection at every instant, and which works in such a way that the instant of disappearance coincides immediately with the appearance of its counterpart. The heart is therefore the center of the Throne and the Throne in its periphery; being the initial point of epiphany, it is also the center which calls into being the space of vision. It is for this reason, says Ḥáfiẓ, that the heart holds the cup of Jam, the cup of cosmic vision, which is also the mirror reflecting the invisible world (*ghayb namá*). But the heart is also ravaged with wounds (*majrúḥ*) as it broods longingly over the stigmata inflicted on it by the Beloved, and acts as a shield against the innumerable arrows that the Beloved's brows let loose. The heart is also purple with the flame of Love and bears as a mark of devotion the "scar of the tulip" (*dagh-i lála*). This scar, says Ḥáfiẓ, "which we have placed in our heart is able to set ablaze the harvest of a hundred rational devout worshippers."

These three essential symbols: the Lord of pre-eternity, the sorrow of love, and the ravaged heart, raise us immediately to the level of the first theophanies, and bring us within the orbit of the famous diving saying according to which God said:

I was a hidden Treasure, I longed to be known.
So I created the creation, in order that I should be known.

God is a Hidden Treasure, that is, an unfathomable essence in the Mystery of Ipseity. But this treasure longs to be known, and initially in His innermost heart a strong desire manifests itself, a nostalgia to reveal Himself; then comes the second stage which fulfills this desire and designates the Names that were concealed in the undifferentiated Thought of God.

Every Name of God aspires to be made manifest, this is what the concept of God's nostalgia and His Love of manifesting himself (*hubb-i huḍúrí*) conveys; it demands an epiphany, a mirror in which it can be reflected: the knower (*'álim*) aspires to be known (*ma'lúm*). This mutual aspiration, this sympathy between Archetypes striving to be invested with the Divine Presence and Names seeking a mirror to contemplate themselves in, constitutes the second visionary theophany (*shuhúdí*), or the marriage of Names and Attributes. But the Archetypes are mirrors of Divine Beauty, and the image reflected in them is the world. To this two-way movement—the longing of the Hidden Treasure to reveal itself in creatures, and the Love of these creatures, aspiring to be united to the Names of which they are epiphanies—correspond the two arcs of descent (*qaws-i nuzúlí*) and ascent (*qaws-i 'urújí*). The descent symbolizes the ceaseless influx of Being; the ascent symbolizing the return movement to God; the former symbolizes the creation in a recurrent and never-failing effusion, the latter the resurrections of beings and their return to their initial and final cause. The cosmic vision of the poet opens into the space between these two arcs, the one originating from the pre-eternity of God (*azal*), and the other starting out from man himself to flow into post-eternity (*abad*).

I. BETWEEN PRE-ETERNITY AND POST-ETERNITY

It is in alluding to this same space between *azal* and *abad* that the poet says:

From the Dawn of the first Beginning till the twilight of the last End,
Friendship and Love have drawn inspiration from one sole pact, one single trust.

Here we enter upon Ḥáfiẓ's visionary topography, we arrive at a world whose co-ordinates are not ordered in the quantitative time of chronological events, and which consequently is neither historical, nor linear, nor progressive, but a world in the interior of which every event is presence, and every duration an instant of this presence. Unquestionably, with regard to the eternity of the Divine itself, the pre-eternal and post-eternal have no meaning, since in its Essence, pre- and post- coincide in the indeterminacy of the divine Ipseity. They take on meaning only in relation to the shadow of God, in relation to that Other-than-He which, while it is a veil obscuring His face, remains no less a necessary expedient of His self-revelation. God and man are the poles of creation; it is between these two poles—one the Origin with regard to descent and the other the Origin with regard to return, that pre- and post-eternity derive all their direction and meaning.

Without the creation of man, who took upon himself the destiny of his folly, there would have been neither initial nor final point, there would have been only the occult eternity of the Hidden Treasure. To see the world as a respite between the initial point and the final point of the cycle of Being is already to anticipate one's return, indeed one's eschatology; it is also to participate in that "play of the magical glance" (*kirishma-i jádú*), in that cycle of love thanks to which the two-way movement of the two arcs developing in opposite directions, sets the cosmic wheel of Being turning. In this state, the poet is established at the center of Being and, as it were, sets the wheel of Love turning. And even while it remains immobile in bewilderment (*sargashta-i pábarjá*) his heart nonetheless spins about in all directions like the needle of a compass. Having become in this way a visionary witness to this play of love, he is the outlet where "the twin tresses of the Eternal Beloved" (*sar-zulfayn-i yár*) are united. It follows that this witnessing is a cosmic vision (*díd-i jahánbín*) which contemplates the play of the cycle of Love turning without respite in the instantaneous succession of a presence that is also, for Ḥáfiẓ, a co-presence in this Play; and a co-attendance at the cosmogonic events of the genesis of the world; that is to say, an act of foundation. For in being present at the first cosmogonic events, the poet is not merely present at these events but, participating in this act, he lays the foundations, through his word, of the world, and assumes a demiurgic role. "Come," he says, "let us split apart the domed ceiling of the celestial spheres, and let us lay the foundation of a new structure." It is by virtue of the nature of this co-presence at, and co-foundation of, the first events that the poet peoples with symbols the visionary space that blossoms, like a primordial lotus, between *azal* and *abad.*

Ḥáfiẓ is unquestionably the most original of all philosophical poets. He never turns his gaze from the primeval focus whence all inspiration comes to him; every glance for him is a glance only insofar as it opens like a magic lamp in the Niche of Prophetic Lights; every drunkenness is drunkenness only insofar as it drinks deep of the wine of the primordial tavern; every head of hair is a head of hair only insofar as the waving chain of its tresses binds up again and commemorates the alliance of the primordial Pact (*'ahd-i alast*); every morning breeze is a breeze only insofar as it brings to us a fragrant breath from the Quarter of the Friend (*kúy-i dúst*). All his attention, his joy, his senses are tense for the space of that unique moment that is granted where every light is a divine theophany, every cup of wine a reflection of the Face of the Beloved, as well as the form of the azure bowl of the sky; every remembrance a reactualization of the primordial memory. His whole soul is present in this sacred space where being is mythogenesis and the *event* an archetypal act in the dawn of the eternal beginning. And it is as a Seer casting his gaze over the "garden of the world" (*bágh-i jahán*) that he would gather, "thanks to the hand of the pupil of his eye, a flower from the Face of the Beloved."

The eye of the poet, illuminated by the eye of the Beloved, sees in this garden the world unveiling itself as the dazzling face of the Beloved, and also becoming clouded over like its dusky hair that darkens its resplendence and makes it appear like "darkened day" (*rúz-i tárík*). This oscillation between Beauty's occultation and self-revelation and its self-revelation and occultation, is conveyed in a number of Ḥáfiẓ's *ghazals* by the "Night of Separation" (*shab-i hijrán*) and the "Day of Union" (*rúz-i waṣl*); for every separation is great with an imminent union, and every union potentially conceals a separation. This succession of repulsion and attraction, which mutually provoke each other, engenders the dialectic movement of Love, and the ascent of nostalgia that permeates all Persian mystical poetry. Here are some examples from Ḥáfiẓ:

> How am I to spread my wing in the span of thy Union,
> For its feathers are shed already in the nest of separation.

And in another place:

In this dark night I have lost the path of the quest.
Come, then, O star that guides us.
Go where I may, my anguish does but grow—
Beware this desert, this endless road.

II. THE AESTHETIC COORDINATES OF THE VISIONARY WORLD

Let us see now how Ḥáfiẓ goes about furnishing this space which opens up between *azal* and *abad*; what, in other words, are the æsthetic consequences of this visionary topography. It goes without saying that we shall scarcely be able to analyze the whole bewitching æsthetic of his poetic world; but we may try to reveal some themes, some modalities of his expression.

Let us say at the outset that the visionary space between *azal* and *abad* comprehends the entire topography of Being itself; that is to say, the ontological hierarchy of the superimposed worlds: the *jabarút* as well as the *malakút*, the world of Archetypal Images, of which Henry Corbin has spoken, as well as the world of sensible phenomena. But for Ḥáfiẓ, who is a mystic and above all a poet, the question is posed not in terms of conceptual explication but in the form of poetic licence, and by the elaboration of a whole magic of symbolic forms suited to convey the polyvalence of what, to the last, remains ineffable, beyond any form of expression. In Ḥáfiẓ, all things come together to translate the untranslatable, to express the inexpressible, and to do this, he has recourse not only to the structure of the *ghazal* itself—which unfolds itself like concentric circles progressively amplifying at each reprise the resonance of spiritual states, and which, because of its drastic limits, demands a polishing of thought to the point of transparency—but Ḥáfiẓ exploits to the full all the virtuosities and subtleties of the Persian language, such as pairs of opposites, correlative terms, word play, homonyms, etymological contrivances, rhythmical alliterations, cadenced assonances, so enhancing the webs of symbols which each reflect.

1) There is in the first place a whole constellation of visual images connected with divine Beauty; symbolized by the most alluring features of

the Eternal Feminine, such as the flowing locks which by a backward movement, like the arc of ascent, bind the lover once more to the initial place where the first knot, the first lock of that hair, is tied; and this lock is an Alliance (*paymán*) that the poet vows never to betray or turn aside from. The eyebrows of the Beloved symbolize sometimes the arched prayer-niche (*miḥráb-i-abrú*); sometimes the bow which lets loose the arrows of her lashes; sometimes the arched roof of the temple of vision of pre-eternity; that is to say, before the ceiling of the vault of heaven had yet been set in its place. The beauty-spot is in keeping with the unitary vision of the world. This "black point" is, the poet says, "but the image of thy beauty-spot in the garden of vision."

Starting from the æsthetic elements of the Eternal Feminine, the visionary topography of the poet is, in broad outline, formed: the topography of the land of the Friend (*kishwar-i dúst*), which has its lanes, its quarters, its prayer-niche, its *ka'ba*, its *qibla*, its hours of contemplation, its garden of ecstasy; whence rises that fine dust which serves as collyrium for his eyes; whence flow the images that throng his imagination; whence rise aloft the messages that come to him, sometimes on the breezes of *ṣabá* (morning) caressing him at the hour of dawn when the candle burns low, sometimes in the cup-bearer's vermilion cup, sometimes in the song of the hoopoe. In Ḥáfiẓ these varied images express the symbol of the divine messenger that we meet again in the form of a youth or angel in the visionary narratives of Avicenna and Suhrawardí; in the form of the Holy Spirit, assimilated to the Active Intelligence in the philosophers; and it is once again the idea of this messenger which is symbolized by the office of mediator that falls to the Angel Gabriel in prophetic revelation. This topography also delineates a whole region of the heart that the poet names *hawá-yi dil* (literally, the weather of the heart), and which constitutes the human configuration of the spiritual realm of *malakút* to which the poet aspires, and in relation to which the world is only an illusion, a snare. Ḥáfiẓ says:

> Her hair is a trap, her beauty-spot the bait in the trap,
> And I in quest of the bait, have fallen into the trap.

2) In its auditory and narrative form, this visionary space is also a story of Love (*qiṣṣa-yi 'ishq*) or the story of a passionate sorrow (*qiṣṣa-yi ghuṣṣa*); an eternal dialogue between lover and Beloved, one and the same

story which is never repeated in exactly the same way, and each narration of which is taken up in a new and hitherto unexpressed form, since it recounts the story of a unique soul in search of its Beloved. Ḥáfiẓ says:

> The nostalgia of Love is always one and the same story,
> But at every hearing it is made new.

But this story goes back to the "story" of an original recital, to a first revelation:

> Behind the mirror I have been made to be like the parrot:
> I repeat what the Lord of pre-eternity has ordered me to say.

Just as every vision is illuminated at the Niche of Prophetic Lights, as every hearing is a hearkening to the original Utterance, as every story of love is a differentiated, particularized version of this same original Utterance, so each presence at the first event is also the remembrance of an alliance whose prolonged echoes constitute the chain of memory, and which the illusory attraction of the world often makes us forget. All of the senses: touch, sight, taste, and, in particular, smell (because the recollective powers of this latter are singularly evocative), are combined in extremely subtle, finely shaded proportions in order to awaken, each in its own way, the memory of the Friend, like the sound of bells of the caravan in the desert, the aromatic musk of the Tartary gazelle, the exquisite aroma of wine, the sweet balm strewn by the messenger wind, so that the fragrant sap of his memory pervades the whole soul of the poem and creates that almost magical space in which images, whatever sensible object they belong to, coincide synchronically to weave the web of this immemorial memory.

3) If the world is impregnated with the memory of the Friend, this memory is also the recollection of a drunkenness, of a cup drunk in pre-eternity within the primordial Tavern:

> Last night I saw the angels knocking at the tavern door,
> Modelling the clay of man, becoming drunk with the original wine;
> The inhabitants of the sacred enclosure and of the divine *malakút*
> Drank from one cup with me, the pilgrim.

If then the angels have mixed the clay of man with the wine of mercy, man carries within himself the quintessence of that first drunkenness and, drinking from the cup in the tavern of the Magi, he does but receive from the cup-bearer what was destined for him from the beginning. But to receive that which was from all time due to us is tantamount to assuming our destiny; it is also tantamount to commemorating the act by virtue of which it was destined for us. It follows from this that the entire universe becomes a tavern fragrant with the wine of merciful Being; and all creatures, all the "drunken ones" of the tavern of the Magi, are like so many cups, and each of them receives, according to the capacity which is his lot, a drop of that delicious drink; and the drunkenness from that drink lasts until the resurrection. As Ḥáfiẓ says:

> Whoever has drunk like me a draught from the cup of the Friend
> Shall not become sober until the dawn of resurrection.

The images relating to the tavern, to cups, to the cup-bearer, are so many symbols which, grafted on to the æsthetic ground of the Eternal Feminine, give rise to this erotico-mystic and Bacchic symbolism of the poet of Shiraz, which is so alluring, and which (alas!) often leads to shallow and hedonist interpretations of his poetry. That there is no antagonism between the earthly wine and the divine wine, just as there is none between profane love and the love of God, since one is the necessary initiation to the other, is what Ḥáfiẓ intends to show. He not only exalts sensible beauty and "earthly nourishment," he transmutes them, thanks to the incantation of his word, into a divine and fantastic banquet at which angels become cup-bearers drunk with love, like those ravishing and lascivious nymphs we admire in the form of *apsáras* in the Buddhist grottoes at Ajanta and Ellora.

4) All these different modalities of sensible expression: sight, hearing, taste, as well as smell, converge, finally, in the memory of an event which is a sort of alliance which itself constitutes man, as well as his destiny. What then is the meaning of this Alliance to which we have referred? Ḥáfiẓ says:

> The heavens could not bear the burden of this Charge (*bár-i amánat*)
> And the winning lot, the Trust, falls to me, the fool.

This Lot is the burden of the Charge (*amánat*) entrusted to man at the beginning; man is, in other words, the repository of the universality of the Names and Attributes, in accordance with this quranic verse, which says:

> We offered [the Trust] to the heavens, to the earth and to the mountains. They refused to take it upon themselves and they were afraid of it; and man assumed it for he is dark (*zalúman*) and ignorant (*jahúlan*). (Qur'án 33:72)

And in the exegesis of the mystics this means: we offered the repository of the universal to Heaven, symbolizing the Spirits, to Earth, representing material bodies, and to the Mountains, symbolizing the world of Archetypal Images; we appealed to their ontological fitness, but they set themselves against it, being unfit to do it, while man had the capacity; that is to say, according to Ḥáfiẓ, he was foolish enough to take on a responsibility that the entire universe refused.

Ḥáfiẓ's openness to the space of memory, as well as his witnessing of events which are so mingled with the mythical dawn of every beginning, work in such a way that the poet, while still in this world, is beleaguered by another world, and while still captive in the snare of illusions, he remains nonetheless the free bird of the garden of visions. This perpetual shuttle between two orders of existence, the one partaking of the free flight of the bird initiated into the "rose-garden of the sacred," and the other mingled with the lamentations of captivity, betrays a paradoxical position which remains inherent in the ambivalent situation of the Seer himself. The poet knows that he belongs to the world of *malakút*, that there is his dwelling-place, the more so as all the epiphanies he contemplates unceasingly invite him there; but he also knows that he has fallen into the cage of earthly existence. Now and then the poet acknowledges his powerlessness to take his flight towards the vertiginous heights.

> How shall I turn within the space of the world of Sanctity
> Since in the alcove of combination [of elements] I remain nailed to my body.

The effect of the oscillating position of Ḥáfiẓ between the world of sanctity and the fall into "time" is that his position expresses on the plane of the spatial movement of the poetic vision that which at the ethical level of *gnosis* remains the paradoxical status of the liberated sage. The poet remains suspended between two manners of apprehending things: having one foot in the other world and one foot in this world; it is with the eschatological bias of the former that he will see this world unfolding itself before his eyes. That is, the time of the poet's presence lies between *abad* and *azal* and is therefore an unveiling; but to this visionary time-space Ḥáfiẓ opposes a horizontal, linear time which runs between the two shores of the world.

From shore to shore the host of darkness stretches,
From *azal* to *abad* opens the dervishes' respite.

His paradoxical situation comes precisely from the crossing of these two times, one of which flows out into post-eternity (*abad*) completing the cycle of Being, while the other establishes the horizon of becoming on the linear plane. It is with regard to this horizontal time that the world is a lure, an illusion, a snare; and to emphasize all this futile trumpery, Ḥáfiẓ uses the image of the new bride.

The world in its outward form is like a new bride,
But whoever cleaves to it offers his life as dowry.

Or again, the world is a ravishing bride, but be warned that this "chaste and modest one becomes the bride of none;" and her infidelity knows no limit. These negative aspects of the world, likened to infidelity, to inconstancy, to the fleeting attractions of a beauty which is, alas, evanescent, are connected with guile, with deceit, because this world, despite being bride (*'arús*), is nonetheless an old woman (*'ajúz*), all wrinkled, full of craft and cunning and who, weaving insidious intrigues, catches creatures in the mesh of her snare; lending herself to all and giving herself to none, "an old woman with a thousand lovers" (*'ajuz-i hazár dámád*). In short, the world is a piece of wizardry, a trick of the conjuror and the illusionist (*shu'bada*). And the more the abyss of this world is revealed to the poet, the more burning becomes his desire to escape from it, and the more raging his thirst to return to his original home.

Where are the tidings of the Union, that I with all my soul may take
the leap?
I am the bird of the Holy places, could I but leap outside the snare of
this world.

This desire for transcendence is at times so irresistible, his ardor so overflowing, that Ḥáfiẓ not only wants to shatter the glass of confinement, to break down the walls of all the prisons, but goes so far as to overstep the frontiers of the resurrection itself, now too narrow to contain the super Abundant ecstasy of a soul who wants to break the cosmic egg, to rend the ceiling of the celestial sphere, "in order to lay there the foundations of a new building."

III. THE PARADOXICAL ETHOS OF THE INSPIRED LIBERTINE (*rend*)

Now what is the ethical behavior of the possessor of the cup of *Jam*? It is here that the notion of *rend* comes in, that untranslatable term that we render indifferently by "inspired libertine," while taking care to underline the inadequacy of this translation; for "the most untranslatable words," says Charles du Bos, "are those that mean most." The word *rend*, as Ḥáfiẓ understands it, sums up the complex and unique traits of the psychology of the Persian. If, in the words of Berdyayev, Dostoevsky illustrates more than any other Russian thinker the "metaphysical hysteria" of the Russian soul, the *rend* of Ḥáfiẓ is the most evocative symbol of the indefinable ambiguity of the Persian character; an ambiguity that often confuses not only Westerners but also the other peoples of the Orient. The term is liable, because of its polyvalent cultural content, to interpretations on many levels, which are often contradictory, indeed paradoxical; all the more so because it implicitly contains its ugly side. These conflicting senses are always resolved when they are reintegrated into the initial constellations to which they all belong.

In this term we find the differing tendencies of the Persian character: its suppleness, its power of adaptation which is not necessarily opportunism, but an art of balance and of "shrinking," as Confucius so aptly put it; however, detached from its original sense, this word can come to mean opportunism. This term also evokes a lively lucidity, a *savoir faire*, a refinement of action, a tact that goes all the way to compliance, a discretion in speech, which are neither craft, nor hypocrisy, nor an affectation of mystery; but can, outside their context, become those very things, being reduced to insidious shifts, not to say to dissembling and imposture. Again, this term denotes an interior liberty, an authentic detachment from the things of this world, suggesting the deliverance, in however small a measure, of the man who lays himself open without shame, naked to the mirror of the world, degenerated from its primitive context, this attitude can turn into one of exhibitionism, of posing, and of mere libertinism. Equally in this concept we find a sense of immoderacy, a behavior out of the ordinary, shocking, scandalous.

This term expresses, further, a predilection for the uncertain, for language that is veiled and masked, for hints and insinuations, which in the authentic *rend* are expressed in inspired paradoxes (*shaṭḥiyát*), in the discipline of the arcane (*taqíya*); but deflected away from its original meaning, it ends in thunderous, puffed-up discourses, and at times in plain falsehood. Finally, there is in this concept a boundless love of the divine such as we see in the great thinkers and mystics of Iranian spirituality; but detached from its mystical content, it is transformed into fanaticism and steered by *homines magni*, to the psychology of the mob. These are the positive qualities of this whole ethic of conduct, almost indecipherable for the non-Persian, with the exception perhaps of the Chinese, that we find in Ḥáfiẓ's concept of *rend.*

The *rend*, annihilated in the Essence and attaining to subsistence in God, is reborn at the level of the first events and rediscovers the world with the eye with which the Hidden Treasure, unveiling itself, brings to light the magical play of its Beauty. This disinterested gaze of the *rend*, which is also the gaze of the Divine itself, Ḥáfiẓ calls *naẓarbáz*; a term every bit as difficult to translate as the word *rend* itself. Translated literally gives, "he who plays with his gaze." In defining his own vision Ḥáfiẓ adds:

> I am the lover (*'áshiq*), the *rend*, the *naẓarbáz*, I own it in all candor,
> That you may know the manifold arts with which I am adorned.

These multiple arts have a common denominator, which is the art *par excellence* of the one possessed of cosmic vision; but they nevertheless express the various modalities of an extremely subtly-shaded truth. Seen from the perspective of dialectic Love, this art is the art of the lover in quest of union with the Beloved; considered from the point of view of ethical conduct it will be simply the art of the inspired libertine, whose provocative, scandalous attitude shocks the narrow-minded, breaking the barren charm of conformity with which people called "rational" hem themselves in; and as seen by the interpreter of the "science of the gaze" (*'ilm-i-naẓar*), this art will be the magical art of "the one who is possessed of the art of the gaze" (*ṣáḥib-i naẓar*).

If the divine face becomes the epiphany of your gaze,
There is no doubt that now you are possessed of the gaze.

To play with one's gaze means not to apprehend the world as an object or an idea, but as an unveiling. Not to see the world as object, is also not to represent it as something out there, laid out in front of us, but to discover it as something opening spontaneously, suddenly before us, like the unveiling within ourselves of a flower in blossom. If the *naẓarbáz* knows and sees that this unfolding is a Play of the divine gaze, it is because his gaze is a Play which has for stake the Play for which the Treasure puts forth its bewitching spell. "It is upon the magical Play of thy gaze," says Ḥáfiẓ, "that we laid the foundation of our being." Now, to be co-witness of the magical play of the divine gaze is also to free oneself from the hold of the two worlds.

I say it in all candor and am pleased with what I say,
Being the slave of Love, I am freed from the two worlds.

It is the union, or the annihilating experience in the Majesty of the essence, and subsistence in its Attributes, which permits the poet to reach the level of the Play, and to be co-witness of the space where this Play unveils itself. It is because of this effacement in this eruption out of the cycle of Being that the poet, tying again the two extremities of the two arcs, in the configuration projected by his gaze, reflects back as the point of coincidence, recomposing and founding again the center and circumference and the pivot which support the axis of the world and the space where the Play of the world opens up. This co-witnessing of the space of the Play is possible only through a surrender of the will, an abandonment to the Play of the divine magic, seeing that it is on the very gratuitousness of this Play that the poet has founded the edifice of his being, and has totally abandoned himself to it.

On the circle of Destiny we are the point of surrender,
That your thought may be all grace, your beginning all order.

If the surrender is an unreserved abandonment to the Play and to the space where this Play unveils itself, it is also, on the plane of consciousness, a non-thought, a stripping away of all that is other than His thought, and on the plane of the will, a non-willing: that is to say, an emptying of all volition which would oppose itself to the bounteous freedom of this Play.

> The thought and will of the self have no existence in our vision [the vision of the *rends*]:
> The vision and will of selfhood are sacrilege in our religion.

It is armed now with this ethic of non-willing, and supplied with the vision of non-thought, which together constitute the true religion of the *rends*, that Ḥáfiẓ so relentlessly unlooses himself, with a rare audacity that makes him one of the greatest protesters in the history of the world against the prohibition-mongers, the inquisitors, the accusers, the preachers, the tradesmen of gnosis, who in the name of symbols devoid of all content, of religion reduced to a commerce in souls, distill the venom of their blindness, who inwardly are as empty as a drum and destitute of all true sorrow. They are precisely the ones who, in making the Qur'án the "snare of hypocrisy" (*dám-i tazwír*), remain outside the religion of love.

> Speak not to the accusers about the mysteries of Love and of drunkenness,
> Since you suffer no pain why do you want Him to heal you?

It is the authenticity of this suffering which binds man to the root of Being, which is lacking in the inconscient (*bí-khabar*), the rationalists (*'áqil*), the false ascetics, the sanctimonious (*záhid*), whose inauthenticity Ḥáfiẓ deplores:

> The inconscient are dumbfounded by the play of our gaze.
> I am as I appear; it is for them to play their role.
> The rationalists are the [fixed] point of the compass of Being,
> But Love knows well that their head turns round within this circle.

The inauthenticity of the "inconscient" is not limited solely to certain individuals but represents an entire category of people who, because they take pleasure in the narrow framework of their "selfhood vision" and believe themselves to be the center of the compass of being, do not know that they are drawn along on it by the whirlwind of Love; in other words, they do not know that it is Love that turns the circle; and so they remain outside that religion of love whose champion Ḥáfiẓ became, pushing to its most extreme consequences a dispute as old as the world; a dispute which has from time immemorial, and particularly in Persian literature, set in opposition the tolerant generosity of the liberated thinker and the obsessional meanness of those who think they possess the truth. Ḥáfiẓ exposes not only a narrow spirit that he styles the narcissistic selfhood-vision, not only a reductionist ethic that he denounces as a snare of hypocrisy, but also and above all a fiction which consists of taking desires for reality.

> Lord forgive the warring of the seventy-two nations,
> For not having seen the truth they have steeped themselves in a fiction.

Fiction (*afsána*) is precisely that screen of prejudices and fixed views which the inconscient project upon the unfathomable depth of what at the deepest level remains a disinterested play of the world: in short all the deceptive appearances which make inauthenticity into a solemn act of self-justification.

In contrast to this, the paradoxical attitude of the *rend* conveys on the ethical, human plane a truth which suffers no limit, no constraint, no repression, be it ever so justified in the eyes of the oldest tradesmen in the world, that is to say religion's prohibition-mongers. Every repression is necessarily a falsehood, a constraint which shackles the spontaneous play of the blossoming of the art of the vision; it is a constraint upon others and upon the censor himself, indeed it is the dark side of that which, driven back, reappears showing its other face:

> Those preachers who from the height of their pulpits sparkle in their sermons,
> When back at home devote themselves to business of a different sort.
> I have a difficulty, and submit it to the wise men of this assembly:
> Those who exhort to penitence, why aren't they penitents themselves?
> One would say that no longer believing in the day of the last judgment,
> They corrupt, by their fraud, the work of the supreme Judge.

To corrupt the work of the supreme Judge is to interfere in the natural course of things, it is to judge men, it is, again, to curtail the free spontaneity of man; for is it not in him that the universality of the divine Names and Attributes is manifested? Who then, Ḥáfiẓ asks us, could "discern good from evil behind the veil (of multiplicity)?" Sin is for the poet never moral vice: it is instead every constraint that encourages falsity, every fetter which would close an interior door, which would level one of the many dimensions of this mystery that is man; which would lead to the trap, to the futility of empty reputation, to the suffocating limits of an idea, to the absence in life of the suffering of Love, to the sclerosis of everyday life; in short, all that could cause us to remain outside that religion of love, that original religion that we receive as the "heritage of our primordial nature" (*míráth-i fiṭrat*). Sin is, in the final reckoning, every action which would betray this primordial nature, which would be false to it, and which would thwart the spontaneous flowering of its Play.

> Though on all sides I am drowned in the sea of sin,
> Being Love's initiate, I am a guest in the house of Mercy.

Let us take an actual example, the closing down of the taverns and the cabarets. This is a so-called hygienic measure which right-minded censors willingly permit themselves in order to reduce sinners to an arid and austere regime of penitence. But this measure has for Ḥáfiẓ a two-fold baneful consequence: it is, on the one hand, the closing of a door and, considering the quality of the man who instigates it, the closing of an interior dimension, reduced now to the "selfhood vision" of the censor's own narrowness of heart; and, on the other hand, this closing necessarily coincides with the opening of another door, which is that of falsity, of deceit, of hypocrisy; and Ḥáfiẓ says in this regard:

> If only the doors of the taverns could be reopened again,
> If only the knots of their repressive measures could be untied.
> If by the blind conceit of the pious they are shut,
> Be patient, for thanks to the love of God they will be opened again.
> By the purity of the rends, these dawn drinkers,
> Numberless doors will be opened by the key of prayers.
> They are closing the doors of the taverns, O my God do not give your
> approval,
> For it is the door of hypocrisy they are opening.

The act as such has no absolute value for Ḥáfiẓ; even blasphemy and sacrilege change their sense according to whether they are envisaged from the point of view of the cosmic vision of the wise man, or from the point of view of the limiting blinkers of the bigots who only project the screen of their own unwillingness; that is to say that every action is bad only if it is grounded in a narrow mind; captive in the nets of the fiction of the world. To the visionary gaze of the *rend*, who is free from all attachment, of all alienating thought, whose heart is polished like a mirror, and who has made his ablutions, like Ḥáfiẓ himself, in the shining spring of Love, wine, for example, not only is not defiling but is rather the elixir of deliverance, and it is in the purple substance of this purifying drink that the poet soaks his prayer-mat. For every inwardly pure being longs for the Friend, it little matters whether he is a sinner or a virtuous man, one who drinks to the dregs, a drunkard or one awakened. And it is also from this original purity that Ḥáfiẓ's tolerance flows: a tolerance which is not to be taken in the usual sense in which we use this word, but which is a deliverance so fundamental, so original, so far removed from the taints and defilements of prejudices, of beliefs, of confessions and of sects, that it appears as a cleansing spring, obliterating at last all the chimeras that men make for themselves

And I shall leave the last word to the poet of Shiraz himself:

> Do not judge the *rends*, you who boast your purity —
> No one will indict you for the faults of others.
> What is it to you whether I am virtuous or a sinner? Busy yourself with yourself!
> Each in the end will reap the seed he himself has sown.
> Every man longs for the Friend, the drunkard as much as the awakened.
> Every place is the House of Love, the Synagogue as much as the Mosque.

Fifty ghazals *from the Díwán of Ḥáfiẓ*

غزل ۱

الا یا ایها الساقی ادر کأساً و ناولها
که عشق آسان نمود اول ولی افتاد مشکلها
ببوی نافه‌ای کاخر صبا زان طرّه بگشاید
ز تاب جعد مشکینش چه خون افتاد در دلها
به می سجاده رنگین کن گرت پیر مغان گوید
که سالک بیخبر نبود ز راه و رسم منزلها
مرا در منزل جانان چه امن عیش چون هر دم
جرس فریاد میدارد که بر بندید محملها
شب تاریک و بیم موج و گردابی چنین هائل
کجا دانند حال ما سبکساران ساحلها
همه کارم ز خودکامی ببدنامی کشید آخر
نهان کی ماند آن رازی کزان سازند محفلها
حضوری گر همی خواهی ازو غائب مشو حافظ
متی ما تلْق من تهوی دع الدنیا و اهملها

Ghazal 1

O Sákí, bring around the cup of wine and then offer it to me,
for love seemed easy at first, but then grew difficult.

Flooded with their heart's blood are those who wait for the scent
that the dawn wind may spill from her dark, musky curls.

Stain your prayer mat with wine if the Magus tells you to,
for such a traveller knows the road, and the customs of its
    stations.

What security is there for us here in her caravanserai
when every moment camel bells cry, "Pack up the loads!"?

The dark night, the fear of waves, the terrifying whirlpool,
how can they know of our state, those who go lightly along the
    shore?

In the end, my life has drawn me from self-concern to ill-repute.
How long can the secret of our assemblies stay hidden?

Ḥáfiẓ, if you desire her presence, pay attention.
When you find the one you seek, abandon the world and let
    it go.

غزل ۲

صلاح کار کجا و من خراب کجا
ببین تفاوت ره کز کجاست تا بکجا
چه نسبتست به رندی صلاح و تقوی را
سماع وعظ کجا نغمهٔ رباب کجا
دلم ز صومعه بگرفت و خرقهٔ سالوس
کجاست دیر مغان و شراب ناب کجا
بشد که یاد خوشش باد روزگار وصال
خود آن کرشمه کجا رفت و آن عتاب کجا
ز روی دوست دل دشمنان چه دریابد
چراغ مرده کجا شمع آفتاب کجا
مبین بسیب زنخدان که چاه در راهست
کجا همی روی ای دل بدین شتاب کجا
چو کُحلِ بینش ماخاک آستان شماست
کجا رویم بفرما ازین جناب کجا
قرار و خواب ز حافظ طمع مدار ای دوست
قرار چیست صبوری کدام و خواب کجا

Ghazal 2

There is the righteous one, here is ruined me.
See how far it is from one to the other!

What link do piety and righteousness have to the rend's way?
There is the sound of the sermon, here is the melody of the rabab.

My heart grew weary of the cloister, the hypocrite's cloak.
Where is the monastery of the Magi? Where is pure wine?

The days of union are gone. Let them be a joyful memory.
Where is that amorous glance? Where is that reproach?

What can the enemy's heart find in my love's face?
There is that dead lamp, here is this sun candle.

Do not be seduced by her dimpled chin, there is a well in that road.
Where are you going, O heart, in such a hurry?

Since the kohl of our insight is the dust of your doorway,
please tell us, where do we go from this threshold?

Do not covet rest and sleep from Ḥáfiẓ, O friend.
What is rest? Which is patience? And where is sleep?

غزل ۳

صبـا بلـطـف بگـو آن غـزال رعنـا را
که سر بکوه و بیابان تو داده‌ای مـا را
شکـر فروش کـه عـمرش دراز بـاد چـرا
تفـقّـدی نکنـد طوطـی شکـرخـا را
چـو بـا حبیـب نشینـی و بـاده پیمـائـی
بیـاد دار مـحـبّان بـاد پیـمـا را
غرور حسن اجـازت مگـر نداد ای گـل
کـه پرسشـی بکنـی عندلیب شیـدا را
بخلق و لطف توان کرد صید اهل نظر
به بنـد و دام نگیـرنـد مرغ دانـا را
نـدانم از چـه سبب رنگ آشنـائـی نیست
سهـی قـدان سیـه‌چشم ماه سیمـا را
جز این قدر نتوان گفت در جمال تو عیب
که وضع مهر و وفا نیست روی زیبا را
در آسمان نه عجب گر بگفتهٔ حافظ
سماع زهره برقص آورد مسیحا را

Ghazal 3

O dawn wind, gently say to that graceful gazelle: 1
"We wander the mountains and desert because of you."

The sugar-seller, long life to him,
why doesn't he ask after the sweet-toothed parrot?

When you sit with the beloved and measure out wine
remember the lovers who measure and drink only wind.

Perhaps your proud beauty keeps you, O rose,
from asking after the frenzied nightingale?

With good nature and kindness one can stalk the insightful ones. 5
The bird of wisdom can't be caught with rope or snare.

I don't know why the tall, dark-eyed, moon-faced ones
bear no trace of friendliness.

One can speak of no fault in your beauty except for this:
there is no affection or loyalty in a lovely face.

In the heavens it's no wonder that when Venus sings Ḥáfiẓ's verse
even the Messiah starts to dance.

غزل ٤

صوفی بیا که آینه صافیست جام را
تا بنگری صفای می لعل فام را
راز درون پرده ز رندان مست پرس
کاین حال نیست زاهد عالی مقام را
عنقا شکار کس نشود دام باز چین
کاینجا همیشه باد بدستست دام را
در عیش نقد کوش که چون آبخور نماند
آدم بهشت روضهٔ دارالسلام را
در بزم دور یک دو قدح در کش و برو
یعنی طمع مدار وصال دوام را
ای دل شباب رفت و نچیدی گلی ز عیش
پیرانه سربکن هنری ننگ و نام را
ما را بر آستان تو بس حقّ خدمتست
ای خواجه بازبین بترحّم غلام را
حافظ مرید جام میست ای صبا برو
وز بنده بندگی برسان شیخ جام را

Ghazal 4

Sufi, the mirror of the cup is clear. Come, 1
and see the purity of this ruby wine.

Ask the drunken rends for the veil's secret,
for this state is not for the "highly ranked" ascetic.

The *'anqá* is no one's prey. Take up your snare,
for here it will find only wind in its grasp.

In life, be content with what you have,
for when the wellspring dried Adam left the garden.

The world and the wine go round. At this banquet 5
drain a bowl or two and go, that is, don't long for eternal life.

O heart, youth has gone, and you didn't pick life's rose.
In old age make something of your name and reputation.

We who have served you have a claim, here, on your threshold.
O lord, look again, with compassion, on your slave.

Ḥáfiẓ is the disciple of the wine cup. O dawn wind, go,
and take my devotion to the Shaikh of Jám.

غزل ۵

ساقی بنور باده برافروز جام ما
مطرب بگو که کار جهان شد بکام ما
ما در پیاله عکس رخ یار دیده ایم
ای بیخبر ز لذّت شرب مدام ما
چندان بود کرشمه و ناز سهی قدان
کآید بجلوه سرو صنوبر خرام ما
هرگز نمیرد آنکه دلش زنده شد بعشق
ثبتست بر جریدهٔ عالم دوام ما
ترسم که صرفه ای نبرد روز بازخواست
نان حلال شیخ ز آب حرام ما
مستی بچشم شاهد دلبند ما خوشست
زانرو سپرده اند بمستی زمام ما
ای باد اگر بگلشن احباب بگذری
زنهار عرضه ده بر جانان پیام ما
گو نام ما ز یاد بعمدا چه می بری
خود آید آنکه یاد نباشد ز نام ما
مستی بچشم شاهد دلبند ما خوشست
زانرو سپرده اند بمستی زمام ما
حافظ ز دیده دانهٔ اشکی همی فشان
باشد که مرغ وصل در آید بدام ما

Ghazal 5

Sákí, make our cup blaze with winelight. 1
Sing, minstrel, the world has become as we wished.

O you who don't understand our joy in perpetual drinking,
in our cup we have seen the image of his face.

There are the winks and flirtations of the slim ones only until
our graceful cypress-pine sways into view.

He whose heart has been revived by love will never die.
In the ledger of the world we are marked "Eternal".

I fear that on Resurrection Day the shaykh's holy bread 5
will be worth no more than our damned wine.

To his eye drunkenness is good,
so they have entrusted our reins to drunkenness.

O wind, if you should pass through the garden of beloveds
be sure to give him our message,

say, "Why do you try to forget our name?
That time when no one can remember will come on its own."

Ḥáfiẓ, keep scattering the grain of your tears,
perhaps the bird of union will fly into our snare.

دریای اخضر فلک و کشتی هلال
هستند غرق نعمت حاجی قوام ما

The green sea of heaven, the hull of the new moon,
are both swamped by the generosity of our Ḥájí Qavám.

غزل ۶

ا نسیـم سحـر آرامگـه یار کـجاسـت
منزل آن مه عاشق کش عیّار کجاست
شب تارست و ره وادی ایمن در پیش
آتش طور کجا موعد دیدار کجاست
هر که آمد بجهان نقش خرابی دارد
در خرابات بگویید که هشیار کجاست
آنکس است اهل بشارت که اشارت داند
نکتها هست بسی محرم اسرار کجاست
هر سر موی مرا با تو هزاران کارست
ما کجاییم و ملامتگر بیکار کجاست
عقل دیوانه شد آن سلسلهٔ مشکین کو
دل ز ما گوشه گرفت ابروی دلدارکجاست
باده و مطرب و گل جمله مهیّاست ولی
عیش بی یار مهیّا نشود یار کجاست
حافظ از باد خزان در چمن دهر مرنج
فکر معقول بفرما گل بی خار کجاست

Ghazal 6

O dawn wind, where is my love's resting-place? 1
Where is the moon's house, that rogue, killer of lovers?

The night is dark, the road to the valley of safety lies ahead.
Where is the fire of Sinai? Where is the moment of meeting?

All who come into this world bear the mark of ruin.
In the tavern ask, "Where is the sober one?"

He who understands signs lives with glad tidings.
There are many subtleties. Where is an intimate of the secrets?

Every tip of our hair has a thousand ties to you. 5
Where are we? And where is the accuser idle?

Reason went mad. Where are those musk-scented chains?
Our heart withdrew from us. Where is the arch of her brow?

Wine, minstrel, and rose are all ready
but there is no pleasure in celebrating without her. Where is she?

Ḥáfiẓ, don't take offense at autumn's wind over the field of the
world.
Think rationally: where is the thornless rose?

غزل ۷

خلوت گزیده را بتماشا چه حاجتست
چون کوی دوست هست بصحرا چه حاجتست
جانا بحاجتی که ترا هست با خدای
کاخر دمی بپرس که ما را چه حاجتست
ای پادشاه حسن خدا را بسوختم
آخر سؤال کن که گدا را چه حاجتست
ارباب حاجتیم و زبان سؤال نیست
در حضرت کریم تمنّا چه حاجتست
محتاج قصّه نیست گرت قصدجان ماست
چون رخت از آن تست بیغما چه حاجتست
جام جهان نماست ضمیر منیر دوست
اظهار احتیاج خود آنجا چه حاجتست
آن شد که بار منّت ملّاح بردمی
گوهر چو دست داد بدریا چه حاجتست
ای عاشق گدا چو لب روح‌بخش یار
میداندت وظیفه تقاضا چه حاجتست
ای مدّعی برو که مرا با تو کار نیست
احباب حاضرند باعدا چه حاجتست
حافظ تو ختم کن که هنر خود عیان شود
با مدّعی نزاع و محاکا چه حاجتست

Ghazal 7

To the recluse, what need is there of entertainment?
In my love's alleyway, who needs scenery?

O beloved, by the need that you have for God,
ask, for a moment, please, what we need.

O king of beauty, by God, we burn.
Ask, please, "What does the beggar need?"

We are rich with need, and have no tongue to ask.
In the presence of God, what need is there of pleading?

If you intend to take our soul there is no need for explanation.
Since our clothes are yours what need is there to plunder?

The world-revealing cup is my love's luminous heart
where there is no need to show your need.

I no longer carry an obligation to the sailor.
Since the pearl has come to hand, who needs the sea?

O beggar lover, when your love's life-giving lip
knows what you need, who needs to ask?

Impostor, go, for we have no business with you.
The friends are here, what need is there of foes?

Finish this, Ḥáfiẓ, to let your talent show.
With the impostor who needs to argue and debate?

غزل ۸

بیا که قصر امل سخت سست بنیادست
بیار باده که بنیاد عمر بر بادست
غلام همّت آنم که زیر چرخ کبود
ز هرچه رنگ تعلق پذیرد آزادست
چگویمت که بمیخانه دوش مست و خراب
سروش عالم غیبم چه مژده ها دادست
که ای بلند نظر شاهباز سدره نشین
نشیمن تو نه این کنج محنت آبادست
ترا ز کنگرهٔ عرش میزنند صفیر
ندانمت که درین دامگه چه افتادست
نصیحتی کنمت یاد گیر و در عمل آر
که این حدیث ز پیر طریقتم یادست
مجو درستی عهد از جهان سست نهاد
که این عجوزه عروس هزار دامادست
غم جهان مخور و پند من مبر از یاد
که این لطیفهٔ عشقم ز ره روی یادست
رضا بداده بده و ز جبین گره بگشا
که برمن و تو در اختیار نگشادست

Ghazal 8

Come, for the palace of hope has weak foundations. 1
Bring wine, for life is built on the wind.

I am the slave of his spiritual power,
he who under this dark blue wheel is untainted by attachment.

What can I tell you but the good news I heard from the invisible world
last night when I sat, drunk and ruined, in the tavern:

"O royal falcon of keen vision, perched in the tree of Heaven,
your nest is not this corner filled with suffering.

They whistle to recall you to the battlements of heaven. 5
I don't understand what has ensnared you here."

I give you some advice; learn it, and in practice remember it,
for it comes from my Master of the Way:

"Do not seek an honest vow from the fickle world,
for this crone is the bride of a thousand men."

Don't fret about the world and don't forget my advice,
for I recall this maxim of love from a fellow traveller:

"Consent to what has been given, and loosen the knot of your brow,
because the door of free will is closed to you and me."

نشان عهد و وفا نیست در تبسم گل
بنال بلبل عاشق که جای فریادست
حسد چه میبری ای سست نظم بر حافظ
قبول خاطر و لطف سخن خدادادست

The rose's smile bears no trace of loyalty or kept promises.
Cry, lover-nightingale, this is the place for it.

O you who build weak verse, why be jealous of Ḥáfiẓ?
To reach the heart, to craft graceful verse, are gifts from God.

غزل ۹

درین زمانه رفیقی که خالی از خللست
صراحی می ناب و سفینهٔ غزلست
جریده رو که گذرگاه عافیت تنگست
پیاله گیر که عمر عزیز بی بدلست
نه من ز بی‌عملی در جهان ملولم و بس
ملالت علما هم ز علم بی‌عملست
بچشم عقل درین ره گذار پر آشوب
جهان و کار جهان بی ثبات و بی محلست
دلم امید فراوان بوصل روی تو داشت
ولی اجل بره عمر رهزن املست
بگیر طرّهٔ مه چهره‌ای و قصّه مخوان
که سعد و نحس ز تأثیر زهره و زحلست
بهیچ دور نخواهید یافت هشیارش
چنین که حافظ ما مست بادهٔ ازلست

Ghazal 9

In these times the only untainted companion left 1
is a cup of clear wine and a book of ghazals.

Go alone, the pass of salvation is narrow.
Take up your glass, there is no substitute for this dear life.

I'm not the only one in the world afflicted with idleness;
the theologians also make no use of their knowledge.

On this turmoil-filled road the eye of reason
knows the world and its handiwork are fleeting and worthless.

My heart longed to see your face 5
but on life's road death plunders the caravans of hope.

Grasp the curl of a moon-faced one and don't claim
that good luck and bad are the work of Venus and Saturn.

Our Ḥáfiẓ is so drunk on the wine of pre-eternity
that in no epoch will you ever find him sober.

غزل ۱۰

زلف آشفته و خوی کرده و خندان لب و مست
پیرهن چاک و غزل خوان و صراحی در دست
نرگسش عربده جوی و لبش افسوس کنان
نیم شب دوش ببالین من آمد بنشست
سر فرا گوش من آورد بآواز حزین
گفت کای عاشق دیرینهٔ من خوابت هست
عارفی را که چنین ساغر شبگیر دهند
کافر عشق بود گر نبود باده پرست
برو ای زاهد و بر دردکشان خرده مگیر
که ندادند جز این تحفه بما روز الست
آنچه او ریخت به پیمانهٔ ما نوشیدیم
اگر از خمر بهشتست و گر از بادهٔ مست
خندهٔ جام می و زلف گره گیر نگار
ای بسا توبه که چون توبهٔ حافظ بشکست

Ghazal 10

Curls dishevelled, sweating, laughing, and drunk, 1
shirt torn, singing ghazals, flask in hand,

his eyes seeking a quarrel, his lips saying, "Alas!",
last night at midnight he came and sat by my pillow.

He bent his head to my ear and said, sadly,
"O my ancient lover, are you sleeping?"

The seeker to whom they give such a cup at dawn
is an infidel to love if he will not worship wine.

O ascetic, go, and don't quibble with those who drink the dregs, 5
for on the eve of Creation this was all they gave us.

What he poured in our cup we drank,
whether the mead of heaven or the wine of drunkenness.

The wine cup's smile and his knotted curl
have broken many vows of repentance, like that of Ḥáfiẓ.

غزل ۱۱

روضهٔ خلد برین خلوت درویشانست
مایهٔ محتشمی خدمت درویشانست
گنج عزّت که طلسمات عجایب دارد
فتح آن در نظر رحمت درویشانست
قصر فردوس که رضوانش بدربانی رفت
منظری از چمن نزهت درویشانست
آنچه زر میشود از پرتو آن قلب سیاه
کیمیائیست که در صحبت درویشانست
آنکه پیشش بنهد تاج تکبّر خورشید
کبریائیست که در حشمت درویشانست
دولتی را که نباشد غم از آسیب زوال
بی تکلّف بشنو دولت درویشانست
خسروان قبلهٔ حاجات جهانند ولی
سببش بندگی حضرت درویشانست
روی مقصود که شاهان بدعا میطلبند
مظهرش آینهٔ طلعت درویشانست
ازکران تا به کران لشکرظلمست ولی
از ازل تا به ابد فرصت درویشانست
ای توانگر مفروش این همه نخوت که ترا
سرو زر در کنف همّت درویشانست

Ghazal 11

The garden of highest Paradise is the dervishes' retreat.
Serving them is the source of magnificence.

The treasure of honor, with its strange talismans,
is won in the merciful gaze of dervishes.

The palace of Paradise, where angels seek to serve,
is but a glimpse from their pleasure-field.

The philosopher's stone that turns the black heart to gold
is the intimacy of dervishes.

The sun dips his crown of grandeur before the greatness
that is found in their retinue.

That wealth which we know can never suffer decay,
listen, simply put, it is the wealth of dervishes.

Kings are the focal point of the world's needs
because they are slaves in the presence of dervishes.

The face that kings desire and seek with prayer
is found in the mirror of their face.

From one border to the other rides the army of cruelty, but
from before creation to beyond time is the domain of dervishes.

O rich one, don't peddle your pride, for your head and your gold
are sheltered by their spiritual power.

گنج قارون که فرو می شود از قهر هنوز
خوانده باشی که هم از غیرت درویشانست
حافظ ار آب حیات ابدی می خواهی
منبعش خاک در خلوت درویشانست
بندهٔ آصف عهدم که درین سلطنتش
صورت خواجگی و سیرت درویشانست

From wrath Qárún's treasure still sinks through the earth.
You may read that this, too, was the zealous work of dervishes.

Ḥáfiẓ, if you want the water of eternal life,
its source is the dust at the doorway of the dervishes' retreat.

I am the slave of Áṣaf, for in this, his reign,
he has the face of a lord and the heart of a dervish.

غزل ۱۲

روزگاریست که سودای بتان دین منست
غم این کار نشاط دل غمگین منست
دیدن روی ترا دیدهٔ جان بین باید
وین کجا مرتبهٔ چشم جهان بین منست
یار من باش که زیب فلک و زینت دهر
از مه روی تو و اشک چو پروین منست
تا مرا عشق تو تعلیم سخن گفتن کرد
خلق را ورد زبان مدحت و تحسین منست
دولت فقر خدایا بمن ارزانی دار
کین کرامت سبب حشمت و تمکین منست
واعظ شحنه شناس این عظمت گو مفروش
زانکه منزلگه سلطان دل مسکین منست
یارب این کعبهٔ مقصود تماشاگه کیست
که مغیلان طریقش گل و نسرین منست
حافظ از حشمت پرویز دگر قصّه مخوان
که لبش جرعه کش خسرو شیرین منست

Ghazal 12

For some time passionate idolatry has been my faith. 1
The pain of this practice is the joy of my sad heart.

One must have a soul-seeing eye to see your face.
How could my world-seeing eye be of this rank?

Be my love, for time's ornaments and heaven's beauty
come from the moon of your face and my tears like the Pleiades.

Ever since my love for you taught me to speak
people always shower me with praise and admiration.

O God, grant me the riches of poverty, 5
for this grace is the source of my dignity, my magnificence.

Preacher, friend to constables, do not peddle this grandeur,
for the house of God is my poor heart.

O Lord, whose garden is this Ka'ba I seek?
The briars of its way are my rose and jonquil.

Ḥáfiẓ, don't tell another story about the pomp of Parviz,
for his lip is but the wine-taster of my sweet king.

غزل ۱۳

خوشتر ز عیش و صحبت و باغ و بهار چیست
ساقی کجاست گو سبب انتظار چیست
هر وقت خوش که دست دهد مغتنم شمار
کس را وقوف نیست که انجام کار چیست
پیوند عمر بسته بموییست هوش دار
غمخوار خویش باش غم روزگار چیست
معنیّ آب زندگی و روضهٔ ارم
جز طرف جویبار و می خوشگوار چیست
مستور و مست هر دو چو از یک قبیله اند
ما دل بعشوهٔ که دهیم اختیار چیست
راز درون پرده چه داند فلک خموش
ای مدّعی نزاع تو با پرده دار چیست
زاهد شراب کوثر و حافظ پیاله خواست
تا در میانه خواستهٔ کردگار چیست

Ghazal 13

What is more joyous than pleasure, intimacy, the garden, and spring? 1
Where is the sákí? Tell me, why are we waiting?

Hoard each joyous moment that comes to you.
No one knows how it all will end.

Our graft to life is tied with a strand of hair. Be aware.
Cry on your own shoulder. What does the world's torment matter?

What is the meaning of the water of life and the garden of Iram
but delicious wine and the edge of this stream?

Since the upright man is kin to the stumbling drunk, 5
to whose sultry glance should we give our heart? What is choice?

What do the heavens know of the veil's secret? O impostor,
be quiet, what is your quarrel with the veil-keeper?

The ascetic thirsts for the wine of Heaven's fountain
and Ḥáfiẓ wants his glass refilled. Which will God prefer?

غزل ۱۴

بحریست بحر عشق که هیچش کناره نیست
آنجا جز آنکه جان بسپارند چاره نیست
هرگه که دل بعشق دهی خوش دمی بود
در کار خیر حاجت هیچ استخاره نیست
فرصت شمر طریقهٔ رندی که این نشان
چون راه گنج بر همه کس آشکاره نیست
ما را بمنع عقل مترسان و می بیار
کان شحنه در ولایت ما هیچ کاره نیست
او را بچشم پاک توان دید چون هلال
هر دیده جای جلوهٔ آن ماه‌پاره نیست
از چشم خود بپرس که ما را که می‌کشد
جانا گناه طالع و جرم ستاره نیست
نگرفت در تو گریهٔ حافظ بهیچ روی
حیران آن دلم که کم از سنگ خاره نیست

Ghazal 14

The sea of love is a sea that has no shore.
There, you can only give up your soul.

Each time you give your heart to love is a joyous moment.
For auspicious deeds there is no need for divination.

Avail yourself of the rend's way, for this mark,
like the road to buried treasure, is not plain to everyone.

Don't frighten us with reason's prohibitions, and bring wine,
for that watchman has no authority in our province.

One can see him with a pure eye, like the new moon.
Not every eye can hold that crescent's beauty.

Ask your own eyes who is killing us. O soul,
it is not the sin of ascendants and the crime of stars.

You are unaffected by the cry of Ḥáfiẓ.
I am perplexed at that heart, hard as granite.

غزل ۱۵

حاصل کارگه کون و مکان این همه نیست
باده پیش آر که اسباب جهان این همه نیست
از دل و جان شرف صحبت جانان غرضست
همه آنست وگرنه دل و جان این همه نیست
منّت سدره و طوبی ز پی سایه مکش
که چو خوش بنگری ای سرو روان این همه نیست
دولت آنست که بی خون دل آید بکنار
ورنه با سعی و عمل باغ جنان این همه نیست
پنج روزی که درین مرحله مهلت داری
خوش بیاسای زمانی که زمان این همه نیست
بر لب بحر فنا منتظریم ای ساقی
فرصتی دان که ز لب تا بدهان این همه نیست
زاهد ایمن مشو از بازی غیرت زنهار
که ره از صومعه تا دیر مغان این همه نیست
نام حافظ رقم نیک پذیرفت ولی
پیش رندان رقم سود و زیان این همه نیست

Ghazal 15

What is made in the workshop of the universe, all this is nothing. 1
Bring out the wine, for the goods of the world are nothing.

Heart and soul seek the honor of intimacy with the beloveds.
That is everything. Otherwise, the heart and soul are nothing.

Don't grow indebted to the trees of Heaven for the sake of shade,
for when you look closely, O flowing cypress, they are nothing.

Good fortune comes without spilling the heart's blood;
otherwise, with effort and practice, Heaven's garden is nothing.

You have five days of respite in this waystation.
Rest easily for a time, because time is nothing. 5

We wait at the edge of the sea's maw of death. O Sákí,
grasp the chance, for from the lip to the mouth is nothing.

Ascetic beware, don't grow complacent in your zealotry,
for the road from your cloister to the Magi's monastery, this is
nothing.

The name of Ḥáfiẓ has become highly distinguished, but
among rends, the distinction between profit and loss is nothing.

غزل ۱٦

دیدی که یار جز سر جور و ستم نداشت
بشکست عهد و ز غم ما هیچ غم نداشت
یارب مگیرش ار چه دل چون کبوترم
افکند و کشت و عزّت صید حرم نداشت
بر من جفا ز بخت من آمد وگرنه یار
حاشا که رسم لطف و طریق کرم نداشت
با این همه هر آنکه نه خواری ازو کشید
هرجا که رفت هیچکسش محترم نداشت
ساقی بیار باده و با محتسب بگو
کانکار ما مکن که چنین جام جم نداشت
هر راهرو که ره بحریم حرم نبرد
مسکین برید وادی و ره در حرم نداشت
حافظ ببر تو گوی فصاحت که مدّعی
هیچش هنر نبود و خبر نیز هم نداشت

Ghazal 16

You saw that my love meant nothing but injustice and abuse? 1
She broke her promise, and our pain caused her no pain.

She threw down and killed my heart, as if it were a pigeon.
O Lord, spare her, although Your law forbids hunting in the
sanctuary.

These misfortunes came to me from my bad luck. Otherwise,
God forbid, she might be thought ungentle or unkind.

Nevertheless, he who never drew her scorn
was not respected, no matter where he went.

Sákí, bring wine, and tell the pious magistrate, 5
"Don't deny us. Not even Jamshid had a cup like this."

Each traveler who didn't find the road to the sacred enclosure
wandered wretched in the desert and never found its door.

Ḥáfiẓ, take the prize for eloquence, for the impostor
had no skill and knew nothing.

غزل ۱۷

شربتی از لب لعلش نچشیدیم و برفت
روی مه پیکر او سیر ندیدیم و برفت
گوئی از صحبت ما نیک بتنگ آمده بود
بار بر بست و بگردش نرسیدیم و برفت
بس که ما فاتحه و حرز یمانی خواندیم
وز پیش سورهٔ اخلاص دمیدیم و برفت
عشوه میداد که از کوی ارادت نرویم
دیدی آخر که چنان عشوه خریدیم و برفت
شد چمان در چمن حسن و لطافت لیکن
در گلستان وصالش نچمیدیم و برفت
همچو حافظ همه شب ناله و زاری کردیم
کای دریغا بوداعش نرسیدیم و برفت

Ghazal 17

We didn't taste a drop from her ruby lip and she left.
We didn't gaze long enough at her beauty and she left.

Perhaps she had tired of our company.
She packed her things, we couldn't overtake her, and she left.

We recited holy suras and blew prayers after her
and she left.

Her sultry glance rooted us in the alley of devotion.
In the end, you saw how deeply we bought that glance, and
she left.

She strolled in the field of grace and beauty but
we didn't go to meet her in the garden of union and she left.

We wailed and wept all night, just like Ḥáfiẓ,
for alas, we were too late to say goodbye and she left.

غزل ۱۸

ساقی بیا که یار ز رخ پرده برگرفت
کار چراغ خلوتیان باز در گرفت
آن شمع سر گرفته دگر چهره برفروخت
وین پیر سالخورده جوانی ز سر گرفت
آن عشوه داد عشق که تقوی ز ره برفت
و آن لطف کرد دوست که دشمن حذر گرفت
زنهار از آن عبارت شیرین دلفریب
گوئی که پستهٔ تو سخن در شکر گرفت
بار غمی که خاطر ما خسته کرده بود
عیسی دمی خدا بفرستاد و بر گرفت
هر سرو قد که بر خور و مه حسن می‌فروخت
چون تو در آمدی پی کاری دگر گرفت
زین قصّه هفت گنبد افلاک پر صداست
کوته نظر ببین که سخن مختصر گرفت
حافظ تو این دعا ز که آموختی که یار
تعویذ کرد شعر ترا و بزر گرفت

Ghazal 18

Sákí come. My love has taken the veil from his face. 1
The light of the solitary ones has been rekindled.

That candle, once beheaded, lit its face again
and burned the grey years from this old man.

Love's sultry glance drove my virtue from the road.
My love was so kind that the enemy stepped aside.

Pay attention to that sweet, charming message.
It is as if your mouth wrapped speech in sugar.

For the burden of grief which struck our heart 5
God sent a messiah who took it away.

Each cypress peddling his beauty to the sun and moon
sat down quietly when you came in.

The seven domes of heaven echo with this story.
Look at the near-sighted who didn't think it worth repeating.

Ḥáfiẓ, from whom did you learn these words, that Fate
has wrapped your verse in gold to wear around its neck?

غزل ۱۹

صبحدم مرغ چمن با گل نوخاسته گفت
ناز کم کن که درین باغ بسی چون تو شکفت
گل بخندید که از راست نرنجیم ولی
هیچ عاشق سخن سخت بمعشوق نگفت
گر طمع داری از آن جام مرصّع می لعل
درّ و یاقوت بنوک مژه‌ات باید سفت
تا ابد بوی محبّت بمشامش نرسد
هر که خاک در میخانه برخساره نرفت
در گلستان ارم دوش چو از لطف هوا
زلف سنبل بنسیم سحری می‌آشفت
گفتم ای مسند جم جام جهان بینت کو
گفت افسوس که آن دولت بیدار بخفت
سخن عشق نه آنست که آید بزبان
ساقیا می ده و کوتاه کن این گفت و شنفت
اشک حافظ خرد و صبر بدریا انداخت
چکند سوز غم عشق نیارست نهفت

Ghazal 19

At dawn the nightingale spoke to the newly-risen rose: 1
"Don't put on airs, for many like you have opened in this
garden."

The rose laughed, "The truth does not offend, but never
has a lover spoken harshly to his love."

If you desire red wine from the jeweled cup
your eyelash must pierce pearl and ruby.

For all eternity the scent of love will elude the one
whose cheek has not swept the dust of the tavern threshold.

Last night in the rosegarden of Iram 5
when a gentle breeze touseled the hyacinth's curls,

I said, "O throne of Jamshid, where is your world-seeing cup?"
It said, "Alas, that bright realm sleeps."

The speech of love is not that which comes to the tongue.
O sákí, give me wine, and cut short this conversation.

The tears of Ḥáfiẓ threw wisdom and patience to the sea.
What to do? Love's burning pain cannot be hidden.

غزل ۲۰

ای هدهد صبا بسبا می فرستمت
بنگر که از کجا بکجا می فرستمت
حیفست طایری چو تو در خاکدان غم
زینجا بآشیان وفا می فرستمت
در راه عشق مرحلهٔ قرب و بعد نیست
می بینمت عیان و دعا می فرستمت
هر صبح و شام قافله ای از دعای خیر
در صحبت شمال و صبا می فرستمت
تا لشکر غمت نکند ملک دل خراب
جان عزیز خود بنوا می فرستمت
ای غایب از نظر که شدی همنشین دل
میگویمت دعا و ثنا می فرستمت
در روی خود تفرّج صنع خدای کن
کآینهٔ خدای نما می فرستمت
تا مطربان ز شوق منت آگهی دهند
قول و غزل بساز و نوا می فرستمت
ساقی بیا که هاتف غیبم بمژده گفت
با درد صبر کن که دوا می فرستمت
حافظ سرود مجلس ما ذکر خیر تست
تعجیل کن که اسب و قبا می فرستمت

Ghazal 20

O hoopoe of the dawn wind, I send you to Sheba. 1
From here, see where I send you!

It's a shame, a bird like you in this crumbling ruin of sorrow.
From here I send you to the nest of loyalty.

On the path of love there is no station of near-and-far.
I can see you clearly, and send off a prayer to you.

Morning and evening I send you a caravan of prayers
as companions of the east wind and the north wind.

Until the army of my sorrow lays waste the kingdom of my heart 5
I will send my dear life to you as a train of provisions.

O hidden one who is now my heart's companion,
I say a prayer to you, I send you greetings;

in your own face view God's creative power
for I send you the God-revealing mirror.

So that the minstrels may tell you of my desire
I send you lyric and ghazal, with music and melody.

Sákí, bring wine, for an invisible voice brought me good news:
"Be patient with pain, for I send you a remedy."

Ḥáfiẓ, our assembly's song is the recollection of your goodness. 10
Hurry up, for I send you a horse and tunic.

غزل ۲۱

ای غایب از نظر بخدا می‌سپارمت
جانم بسوختی و بدل دوستدارمت
تا دامن کفن نکشم زیر پای خاک
باور مکن که دست ز دامن بدارمت
محراب ابروان بنما تا سحر گهی
دست دعا بر آرم و در گردن آرمت
گر بایدم شدن سوی هاروت بابلی
صد گونه جادوئی بکنم تا بیارمت
خواهم که پیش میرمت ای بی‌وفا طبیب
بیمار باز پرس که در انتظارمت
صد جوی آب بسته‌ام از دیده بر کنار
بر بوی تخم مهرکه در دل بکارمت
خونم بریخت وز غم عشقم خلاص داد
منّت پذیر غمزهٔ خنجر گذارمت
بارم ده از کرم سوی خود تا بسوز دل
در پای دم بدم گهر از دیده بارمت
حافظ شراب و شاهد و رندی نه وضع تست
فی‌الجمله میکنی و فرو میگذارمت

Ghazal 21

O invisible one, I entrust you to God. 1
You burned my soul and with my heart I love you.

Until I drag the hem of my shroud under the earth
don't believe I will ever let go of the hem of your skirt.

Show me the arched niche of your eyebrows so that at dawn
I may raise my arms in prayer and clasp your neck.

Even if, like Hárút, I must be hung by my feet,
I will cast a hundred spells to conjure you.

I want to die near you. O faithless healer, 5
visit the sick one again, I am waiting.

I have cried a hundred streams across my breast
hoping to water the seed of kindness in your heart.

My spilled blood freed me from the pain of love.
I am grateful to the dagger of your glance.

Be kind, grant me an audience, so that with burning heart
my eyes can constantly rain pearls at your feet.

Ḥáfiẓ, wine and the beloved and the rend's way are not for you,
but you pursue them all and I overlook it.

غزل ۲۲

روز وصـــل دوســـتـداران یاد باد
یاد باد آن روزگـاران یاد باد
کامم از تلخی غم چون زهرگشت
بانگ نوش شاد خواران یاد باد
گـرچـه یاران فـارغنـد از یاد مـن
از من ایشانـرا هزاران یاد باد
مبتـلا گشـتم دریـن بنـد و بلا
کوشش آن حق گزاران یاد باد
گرچه صد رودست درچشمم مدام
زنده رود و باغکـاران یاد باد
راز حافظ بعد ازین ناگفته ماند
ای دریغ آن رازداران یاد باد

Ghazal 22

Remember the day of union with the friends. 1
Remember those times, remember.

From bitter sorrow my mouth became like poison.
Remember the revelers' cry of "Drink!"

The friends are free of the memory of me
although I remember them a thousand times.

I was overtaken in these bonds of calamity.
Remember the efforts of those who serve the truth.

Although there are always a hundred rivers in my eye 5
remember the Zindehrúd, and those who plant gardens.

After this Ḥáfiẓ's secret will remain unspoken.
Alas, remember those who keep the secrets.

غزل ۲۳

هر آنکه خاطری مجموع و یاری نازنین دارد
سعادت همدم او گشت و دولت همنشین دارد
حریم عشق را درگه بسی بالاتر از عقلست
کسی آن آستان بوسد که جان در آستین دارد
دهان تنگ شیرینت مگر مهر سلیمانست
که نقش خاتم لعلش جهان زیر نگین دارد
لب لعل و خط مشکین چو آنش هست اینش نیست
بنازم دلبر خود را که حسنش آن و این دارد
چو بر روی زمین باشی توانائی غنیمت دان
که دوران ناتوانیها بسی زیر زمین دارد
بخواری منگر ای منعم ضعیفان و نحیفانرا
که صدر مجلس عزّت فقیر رهنشین دارد
بلاگردان جان و تن دعای مستمندانست
که بیند خیر از آن خرمن که ننگ ازخوشه چین دارد
صبا از عشق من رمزی بگو با آن شه خوبان
که صد جمشید و کیخسرو غلام کمترین دارد
اگر گوید نمیخواهم چو حافظ عاشقی مفلس
بگوئیدش که سلطانی گدائی همنشین دارد

Ghazal 23

Everyone who has a clear mind and a lovely friend
is an intimate of bliss and a companion to good fortune.

The threshold of love's sanctuary lies above that of reason.
To kiss that threshold you must be ready to scatter your life like
coins.

Is your small, sweet mouth the seal of Solomon?
The image on its ruby bezel rules all the world.

The boy with ruby lips lacks a darkening beard.
I boast of my beloved. He has both.

Do as much as you can while you walk the earth,
for under the earth time holds many who can do nothing.

O rich one, do not look with contempt on the weak and feeble,
for in the assembly's seat of honor sits the roadside pauper;

the prayers of the needy keep disaster from soul and body,
will you see a full harvest if you scorn the gleaners?

Wind, tell a secret of my love to that king of beauties,
who among his slaves has a hundred Khusraus and Jamshids,

and if he says, "I do not want a poor lover like Ḥáfiẓ,"
tell him that true kings sit with wandering beggars.

غزل ٢٤

سالها دل طلب جام جم از ما میکرد
و آنچه خود داشت ز بیگانه تمنّا میکرد
گوهری کز صدف کون و مکان بیرونست
طلب از گمشدگان لب دریا میکرد
مشکل خویش بر پیر مغان بردم دوش
کو بتائید نظر حلّ معمّا میکرد
دیدمش خرّم و خندان قدح باده بدست
و اندر آن آینه صد گونه تماشا میکرد
گفتم این جام جهان بین بتوکی داد حکیم
گفت آن روز که این گنبد مینا میکرد
گفت آن یار کزو گشت سردار بلند
جرمش این بود که اسرار هویدا میکرد
بیدلی در همه احوال خدا با او بود
او نمیدیدش و از دور خدایا میکرد
این همه شعبدهٔ عقل که میکرد اینجا
سامری پیش عصا و ید بیضا میکرد
فیض روح القدس ار باز مدد فرماید
دیگران هم بکنند آنچه مسیحا میکرد
گفتمش سلسلهٔ زلف بتان از پی چیست
گفت حافظ گله ای از دل شیدا میکرد

Ghazal 24

For years my heart asked me for Jamshid's cup. 1
That which it held it sought from a stranger.

It sought the pearl that lies outside the world's shell
from the lost ones at the edge of the sea.

Last night I took my dilemma to the Magus
so that with his vision he could find the answer.

I saw him joyous, laughing, cup in hand,
and in that mirror one could see a hundred images.

I said, "When did God give you this world-seeing cup?" 5
He said, "The day that He built this dark blue dome."

He said, "That beloved who raised up the gallows,
his sin was this: he spilled the secrets.

In all states God walked with the lost-hearted,
who saw nothing and into the distance called, 'O God!'

All the sleights-of-hand with which reason tricks us here
the sorcerers tried before Moses, to no avail.

If the grace of the Holy Spirit helps again
others may raise the dead as Jesus did."

I asked, "The chains of the idol's hair, what are they for?" 10
He said, "Ḥáfiẓ complained of a frenzied heart."

غزل ۲۵

بسرّ جام جم آنگه نظر توانی کرد
که خاک میکده کحل بصر توانی کرد
مباش بی می و مطرب که زیر طاق سپهر
بدین ترانه غم از دل بدر توانی کرد
گل مراد تو آنگه نقاب بگشاید
که خدمتش چو نسیم سحر توانی کرد
گدائی در میخانه طرفه اکسیریست
گر این عمل بکنی خاک زر توانی کرد
جمال یار ندارد نقاب و پرده ولی
غبار ره بنشان تا نظر توانی کرد
بعزم مرحلهٔ عشق پیش نه قدمی
که سودها کنی ار این سفر توانی کرد
تو کز سرای طبیعت نمی روی بیرون
کجا بکوی طریقت گذر توانی کرد
دلا ز نور هدایت گر آگهی یابی
چو شمع خنده زنان ترک سر توانی کرد
ولی تو تا لب معشوق و جام می خواهی
طمع مدار که کار دگر توانی کرد
گر این نصیحت شاهانه بشنوی حافظ
بشاهراه حقیقت گذر توانی کرد

Ghazal 25

You can see the secret of Jamshid's cup
the moment you can make tavern dust into the kohl of sight.

Don't be without wine and minstrel, for under the sky's arch
with this song you can banish pain from your heart.

The rose of your desire will lift its veil
the moment you can serve it like the wind of dawn.

Begging at the tavern door is a rare elixir.
If you do this you can turn dust to gold.

My love's beauty has no mask, no veil, but
let the road's dust settle, so you can see.

With your eye on the waystation of love, step forward;
you will reap profit if you can make this journey.

You who never leave the walled house of your nature,
how can you pass through the alley of the Way?

O heart, if you become aware of the light that guides
like the laughing candle you can give up your head,

but as long as you want his lips and the wine cup
don't imagine that you can do anything else.

If you listen to this royal advice, Ḥáfiẓ,
you can travel the royal road of truth.

غزل ۲۶

در ازل پرتو حسنت ز تجلّی دم زد
عشق پیدا شد و آتش به همه عالم زد
جلوه‌ای کرد رخت دید ملک عشق نداشت
عین آتش شد ازین غیرت و بر آدم زد
عقل می‌خواست کزان شعله چراغ افروزد
برق غیرت بدرخشید و جهان بر هم زد
مدّعی خواست که آید به تماشاگه راز
دست غیب آمد و بر سینهٔ نامحـــرم زد
دیگران قرعهٔ قسمت همه بر عیش زدند
دل غمدیدهٔ ما بود که هـم بر غـــم زد
جان علوی هوس چاه زنخدان تو داشت
دست در حلقهٔ آن زلف خم اندر خم زد
حافظ آن روز طربنامهٔ عشق تو نوشت
کــه قلم بـــر سر اسباب دل خرّم زد

Ghazal 26

On the eve of Creation the ray of your beauty broke forth. 1
Love appeared, and fire burned all the world.

The radiance of your face appeared. Incensed that the angel
could not love,
it became the essence of fire and struck Adam.

With that flame reason sought to light a lamp.
Your zeal was bolt lightning, and stirred up all the world.

The impostor came to see the secret. He was not kin,
and the hand of the invisible pushed him away.

All the others cast their lots for pleasure. 5
Our pain-filled heart was the one that cast its lot for sorrow.

The celestial soul sought to drink from the well of your dimple,
and lowered himself on the curved curls of your hair.

Ḥáfiẓ finished his book on the joy of loving you
the day that he crossed out all that describes a cheerful heart.

غزل ۲۷

اگر روم ز پیش فتنه ها برانگیزد
ور از طلب بنشینم بکینه بر خـــیزد
وگر برهگذری یکدم از وفاداری
چو گرد در پیش افتم چو باد بگریزد
وگر کنم طلب نیم بوسه صد افسوس
ز حقّهٔ دهـنش چون شکـر فرو ریـزد
من آن فریب که در نرگس تو میبینم
بس آبروی که با خـک ره بر آمیـزد
فراز و شیب بیابان عشق دام بلاست
کجاســت شیردلی کـز بـلا نـپرهیـزد
تو عمر خواه و صبوری که چرخ شعبده باز
هـزار بـازی ازین طـرفه تر بر انگیزد
بـر آستانهٔ تسلیم سـر بنـه حافـظ
که گر ستیزه کنی روزگار بستیزد

Ghazal 27

If I follow her, she stirs up trouble;
and if I sit back, she rises up in anger;

and if on a road, for one moment, in my loyalty,
like dust I follow her, like wind she flees;

and if I seek half a kiss from the jewel-box of her mouth,
hundreds of "So sorry!"s spill down like sugar.

That deceit which I see in your eyes
muddies many a good name with the dust of the road.

The hills and valleys of love's wilderness are the snare of affliction.
Who has a lion's heart, and will not shun affliction?

Seek life and patience, for the great wheel, with its sleight-of-
hand,
has a thousand tricks more strange than these.

Ḥáfiẓ, place your head on the threshold of submission,
for if you argue, fate will argue back.

غزل ۲۸

هر که شد محرم دل در حرم یار بماند
وانـکه ایـن کار ندانست در انکار بماند
اگر از پرده برون شد دل من عیب مکن
شکـر ایزد کـه نه در پـردهٔ پندار بـماند
صوفیان واستدند از گرو می همه رخت
دلـق ما بود کـه در خـانهٔ خـمّار بـماند
خرقه‌پوشان دگر مست گذشتند و گذشت
قصّهٔ ماسـت کـه در هـر سر بازار بـماند
هر می لعل کز آن دست بلورین ستدیم
آب حسرت شد و در چشم گهر بار بماند
جز دل من کز ازل تا بابد عاشق اوست
جـاودان کس نشنیدیم کـه در کار بـماند
از صدای سخن عشق ندیدم خوشتر
یـادگـاری کـه دریـن گنبـد دوّار بـماند
گشت بیمار که چون چشم تو گردد نرگس
شیـوهٔ تو نـشدش حـاصل و بیمـار بـماند
بتماشا گـه زلفش دل حافـظ روزی
شد که باز آید و جاوید گرفتار بماند

Ghazal 28

Each one who became an intimate of the heart remained in my
love's sanctuary,
and the one who didn't understand this remained in denial.

Don't fault my heart if it shed the veil.
Thank God it didn't stay veiled in its imagination.

The Sufis redeemed all the clothes they pawned for wine.
Only our coat remained in the tavern.

The other Sufis passed by drunk and no one noticed.
Only our story remained the talk of every bazaar.

The ruby wine that we took from that pale hand
turned to pure regret and remained in our eyes like pearls.

My heart has been his lover from before creation to beyond time.
We have heard of no one else who has been eternal in this work.

I have never seen a more beautiful reminder
than the words of love that linger in this turning dome.

The narcissus tried to mimic your sultry eyes.
Your ways were beyond him, and he lies sick still.

One day Ḥáfiẓ's heart went to gaze at his lovely curls.
It meant to return but remained entangled forever.

غزل ۲۹

دوش دیدم که ملایک در میخانه زدند
گل آدم بسرشتند و به پیمانه زدند
ساکنان حرم ستر و عفاف ملکوت
با من راه‌نشین بادهٔ مستانه زدند
آسمان بار امانت نتوانست کشید
قرعهٔ کار بنام من دیوانه زدند
جنگ هفتاد و دو ملّت همه را عذر بنه
چون ندیند حقیقت ره افسانه زدند
شکر ایزد که میان من و او صلح افتاد
قدسیان رقص‌کنان ساغر شکرانه زدند
ما بصد خرمن پندار ز ره چون نرویم
چون ره آدم بیدار بیک دانه زدند
آتش آن نیست که بر شعلهٔ او خندد شمع
آتش آنست که در خرمن پروانه زدند
کس چو حافظ نکشید از رخ اندیشه نقاب
تا سر زلف سخن را بقلم شانه زدند

Ghazal 29

Last night I saw angels knock on the tavern door. 1
They kneaded the clay of Adam and molded it into a cup.

Those who live in the veiled and chaste sanctuary of Heaven
drank strong wine with me, the wandering beggar.

The sky couldn't bear the burden of His trust,
so they cast lots and drew the name of crazy me.

Excuse all the seventy-two nations at war.
They did not see the truth, and took the road of fable.

Thank God that peace has fallen between us. 5
The celestials danced and drank the cup of gratitude.

How can we not be diverted by a thousand thoughts
when they waylaid watchful Adam with a single grain?

Fire is not that at which the candle laughed.
Fire is that with which they struck the tinder of the moth.

No one has unveiled the face of thought as well as Ḥáfiẓ
since men began to comb, with a pen, the curly hair of speech.

غزل ۳۰

سمن بویان غبار غم چو بنشینند بنشانند
پری رویان قرار از دل چو بستیزند بستانند
بفتراک جفا دلها چو بر بندند بر بندند
ز زلف عنبرین جانـها چو بگشایند بفشانند
بعمری یک نفس با ما چو بنشینند بر خیزند
نهال شوق در خاطـر چو بـر خیزند بنشانند
ز چشم لعل رمّانی چو میبارند میخندند
ز رویـم راز پنـهانی چو میبینند مـیخواننـد
سرشک گوشه گیران را چو دریابند دریابند
رخ از مهر سحر خیزان نگردانند اگر دانند
دوای درد عاشق را کسی کو سهل پندارد
ز فـکر آنان کـه در تدبیر درمـانند درمانند
چو منصور از مراد آنان که بردارند بردارند
بدین درگاه حافـظ را چو میخوانند مـیرانند

Ghazal 30

When the jasmine-scented ones sit down they settle the dust of sorrow.
When the fairy-faced ones quarrel they steal peace from the heart.

When they ride they strap our hearts to their saddle with capriciousness.
When they let down their perfumed hair they scatter souls.

When they sit with us one moment in a lifetime they get up.
When they get up they root saplings of longing in the heart.

When they make my eyes rain pomegranate tears they laugh.
When they look they read the hidden secret in my face.

When they discover the tears of the secluded ones they see pearls.
When they understand, they do not turn their face from the love of those who rise at dawn.

Whoever thinks the lover's pain has an easy cure
will be paralyzed by searching for a remedy.

Those whose desires bear fruit, like Ḥalláj, stand upon the gallows.
Whenever they call Ḥáfiẓ to this threshold they send him away.

غزل ۳۱

واعظان کین جلوه در محراب و منبر میکنند
چون بخلوت میروند آن کار دیگر میکنند
مشکلی دارم ز دانشمند مجلس باز پرس
توبه فرمایان چرا خود توبه کمتر میکنند
گوئیا باور نمی دارند روز داوری
کین همه قلب و دغل در کار داور میکنند
بندهٔ پیر خراباتم که درویشان او
گنج را از بی‌نیازی خاک بر سر میکنند
یارب این نو دولتانرا بر خر خودشان نشان
کین همه ناز از غلام ترک و استر میکنند
بر در میخانهٔ عشق ای ملک تسبیح گوی
کاندر آنجا طینت آدم مخمّر میکنند
حسن بی پایان او چندانک عاشق می کشد
زمرهٔ دیگر بعشق از غیب سر بر میکنند
ای گدای خانقه باز آ که در دیر مغان
میدهند آبی که دلها را توانگر میکنند
خانه خالی کن دلا تا منزل جانان شود
کین هوسناکان دل و جان جای لشکر میکنند
صبحدم از عرش می‌آمد خروشی عقل گفت
قدسیان گویی که شعر حافظ از بر میکنند

Ghazal 31

Preachers who display their piety in prayer and pulpit
behave differently when they're alone.

It puzzles me. Ask the learned ones of the assembly:
"Why do those who demand repentance do so little of it?"

It's as if they don't believe in the Day of Judgment
with all this fraud and counterfeit they do in His name.

I am the slave of the tavern-master, whose dervishes,
in needing nothing, make treasure seem like dust.

O lord, put these nouveaux-riches back on their asses
because they flaunt their mules and Turkic slaves.

O angel, say praises at the door of love's tavern,
for inside they ferment the essence of Adam.

Whenever his limitless beauty kills a lover
others spring up, with love, from the invisible world.

O beggar at the cloister door, come to the monastery of the
Magi,
for the water they give makes hearts rich.

Empty your house, O heart, so that it may become home to the
beloved,
for the heart of the shallow ones is an army camp.

At dawn a clamor came from the throne of heaven. Reason said,
"It seems the angels are memorizing Ḥáfiẓ's verse."

غزل ۳۲

سالها دفتر ما در گرو صهبا بود
رونـق مـیکده از درس و دعـای مـا بـود
نیکی پیر مغان بین که چو ما بدمستان
هـر چـه کردیـم بچشم کـرمش زیبا بـود
دفتر دانش ما جمله بشوئید بمی
کـه فلک دیـدم و در کـین مـن دانا بود
از بتان آن طلب ار حسن شناسی ای دل
کاین کسی گفت که در علم نظر بینا بود
دل چو پرگار بهر سو دورانی میکرد
وانـدر آن دایـره سـرگشتـهٔ پـا بـرجا بود
مطرب از درد محبّت عملی میپرداخت
کـه حـکیمان جـهان را مژه خون پالا بود
میشکفتم ز طرب زآنک چو گل بر لب جوی
بـر سرم سـایهٔ آن سـرو سهـی بـالا بـود
پیر گلرنگ من اندر حق ازرق پوشان
رخـصت خبث نـداد ارنـه حـکایتهـا بـود
قلب اندودهٔ حافظ بر او خرج نشـد
که معامل بهمه عیب نهان دانا بود

Ghazal 32

For years our notebook was pawned for wine. 1
The tavern's lustre came from our lessons and prayer.

See the goodness of the Magus, for as we staggered, drunk,
his generous eye saw beauty in whatever we did.

Wash all the notebook of our wisdom clean with wine,
for I have seen the heavens, and they lie in wait for clever me.

O heart, if you know beauty, seek its essence from the idols,
for this was said by someone who could see through chapter
    and verse.

5

Like a compass, the heart spun in all directions,
and bewildered, stood firmly in that circle.

The minstrel played improvisations on the pain of love
so that the wise ones of the world shed tears of blood.

Like the rose at the stream's edge I blossomed with joy,
for I lay in the shadow of that tall cypress.

My rose-colored master would hear no malice against his
    blue-clad disciples,
otherwise much would have happened;

and this merchant did not spend the counterfeit heart of Ḥáfiẓ
because he was wise to every hidden fault.

غزل ۳۳

تا ز میخانه و می نام و نشان خواهد بود
سر ما خاک ره پیر مغان خواهد بود
حلقهٔ پیر مغان از ازلم در گوشست
بر همانیم که بودیم و همان خواهد بود
بر سر تربت ما چون گذری همّت خواه
که زیارتگه رندان جهان خواهد بود
برو ای زاهد خودبین که ز چشم من و تو
راز این پرده نهانست و نهان خواهد بود
ترک عاشق‌کش من مست برون رفت امروز
تا دگر خون که از دیده روان خواهد بود
چشمم آن شب که ز شوق تو نهم سر بلحد
تا دم صبح قیامت نگران خواهد بود
بخت حافظ گر ازین گونه مدد خواهد کرد
زلف معشوقه بدست دگران خواهد بود

Ghazal 33

As long as the wine and tavern exist
our head will be dust on the Magus's road.

His slave-ring has been in our ear since before Creation.
As we were then, we are and will always be.

When you pass by our tomb wish for spiritual power,
for to the rends of the world it will be a place of pilgrimage.

O self-seeing ascetic, go, because from your eyes and mine
the veil's secret is hidden, and will always be hidden.

My Turk, that killer of lovers, went out drunk today;
who else will feel the blood flow from his eyes?

From that night when I lay my head on my tomb for you
my eye will peer anxiously until the dawn of Resurrection.

If Ḥáfiẓ's luck provides this kind of help
the beloved's hair will run through the fingers of others.

غزل ٣٤

گر من از باغ تو یک میوه بچینم چه شود
پیش پایی بچراغ تـو ببینم چه شود
یارب اندر کنف سایهٔ آن سرو بلند
گر من سوخته یکدم بنشینم چه شود
آخر ای خاتم جمشید همایون آثار
گر فتد عکس تو بر لعل نگینم چه شود
واعظ شهر چو مهر ملک و شحنه گزید
من اگر مهر نگاری بگزینم چه شود
عقلم از خانه بدر رفت و گر می اینست
دیدم از پیش که در خانهٔ دینم چ شود
صرف شد عمر گرانمایه به معشوقه و می
تا از آنم چه پیش آید ازینم چه شود
خواجه دانست که من عاشقم و هیچ نگفت
حافظ ار نیز بداند که چنینم چه شود

Ghazal 34

If I pick one fruit from your garden, what does it matter? 1
If I take a step by the light of your lamp, what does it matter?

O lord, if, for one moment, my burning self sits
in the shade of that tall cypress, what does it matter?

O seal of auspicious Jamshid, if your image should, at last,
fall on my ruby bezel, what does it matter?

The city preacher chose the affection of king and constable.
If I choose the affection of a slender beauty, what does it
matter?

My reason fled its house, and if this is wine's work, 5
From what I've seen, what will happen to the house of my faith?

I spent my precious life on the beloved and on wine.
Let's see what will come to me from the one, and from the
other.

The lord knew I was a lover and said nothing.
If Ḥáfiẓ knows this also, what does it matter?

غزل ۳۵

گفتم غم تو دارم گفتا غمت سر آید
گـفتم کـه مـاه من شو گفتا اگر بر آید
گفتم ز مهرورزان رسم وفا بیاموز
گـفتا ز مـاهرویان ایـن کـار کمتر آید
گفتم که بر خیالت راه نظر ببندم
گفتا که شبرو است او از راه دیگر آید
گفتم که بوی زلفت گمراه عالمم کرد
گـفتا اگـر بدانی هـم اوت رهبر آید
گفتم خوشا هوایی کز باغ حسن خیزد
گـفتا خنک نسیمی کـز کوی دلبر آید
گفتم که نوش لعلت ما را بآرزو کشت
گـفتا تـو بندگی کن کو بنده پرور آید
گفتم دل رحیمت کی عزم صلح دارد
گـفتا مگوی بـا کس تا وقت آن بر آید
گفتم زمان عشرت دیدی که چون سر آمد
گفتا خموش حافظ کین غصه هم سر آید

Ghazal 35

I said, "I suffer because of you." She said, "Your suffering will end." 1
I said, "Become my moon." She said, "If it comes to pass."

I said, "From lovers learn the custom of loyalty."
She said, "Among moon-faced ones this is rarely found."

I said, "I will barricade your image from the road of my sight."
She said, "It is a thief, and will come a different way."

I said, "The scent of your hair has led me astray in the world."
She said, "If you understand, it can also be your guide."

I said, "Happy is the wind that rises from the garden of beauty." 5
She said, "Fresh is the breeze that comes from my alleyway."

I said, "Thirst for your ruby lip killed us with hope."
She said, "Serve it, for it comes to nourish its servants."

I said, "When does your merciful heart intend a truce?"
She said, "Speak of this to no one until that time comes."

I said, "Did you see how those joyful times ended?"
She said, "Be quiet, Ḥáfiẓ. This grief will also end."

غزل ۳۶

صبا ز منزل جانان گذر دریغ مدار
و زو بعاشق مسکین خبر دریغ مدار
بشکر آنکه شکفتی بکام دل ای گل
نسیم وصل ز مرغ سحر دریغ مدار
حریف عشق تو بودم چو ماه نو بودی
کنون که ماه تمامی نظر دریغ مدار
کنون که چشمهٔ قندست لعل نوشینت
سخن بگوی و ز طوطی شکر دریغ مدار
جهان و هرچه درو هست سهل و مختصر ست
ز اهل معرفت این مختصر دریغ مدار
مکارم تو بآفاق میبرد شاعر
ازو وظیفه و زاد سفر دریغ مدار
چو ذکر خیر طلب میکنی سخن اینست
که در بهای سخن سیم و زر دریغ مدار
غبار غم برود حال خوش شود حافظ
تو آب دیده ازین رهگذر دریغ مدار

Ghazal 36

O wind, don't refuse to pass by the house of the beloved, 1
and don't keep news of her from the poor lover.

O rose, you unfolded as your heart desired. In gratitude,
don't keep the wind of union from the bird of dawn.

When you were a new moon I was your love's companion.
Now that you are a full moon don't withold your glance.

Now that your sweet ruby lip is the source of sugar,
speak, and don't keep sugar from the parrot.

This world, with all it contains, is slight and brief. 5
Don't keep this trifle from people of insight.

The poet carries your generosity to all horizons.
Don't refuse him compensation and provisions for his journey.

If you seek to be well-remembered, there is a saying:
"When you value verse, don't hold back gold and silver."

The dust of sorrow will subside. Happiness will come.
Ḥáfiẓ, don't keep your tears from this roadway.

غزل ۳۷

الا ای طوطی گویای اسرار
مبادا خالیت شکّر ز منقار
سرت سبز و دلت خوش باد جاوید
که خوش نقشی نمودی از خط یار
سخن سربسته گفتی با حریفان
خدا را زین معمّا پرده بردار
بروی ما زن از ساغر گلابی
که خواب آلوده ایم ای بخت بیدار
چه ره بود این که زد در پرده مطرب
که میرقصند با هم مست و هشیار
ازین افیون که ساقی در می افکند
حریفانرا نه سر ماند نه دستار
سکندر را نمی بخشند آبی
بزور و زر میسّر نیست این کار
خرد هرچند نقد کایناتست
چه سنجد پیش عشق کیمیاگار
بیا و حال اهل درد بشنو
بلفظ اندک و معنیّ بسیار
بت چینی عدوی دین دلهاست
خداوندا دل و دینم نگهدار

Ghazal 37

Ho, O parrot, speaker of secrets!
May your beak never lack sugar!

May you live long, may your heart be happy forever,
for you have shown us a lovely image of his figure.

You spoke in riddles with the companions.
For God's sake, lift the veil from this enigma.

O bright luck, splash our face with rosewater,
for we are stained with sleep.

What melody did the minstrel play
that the drunk and sober dance together?

Because the sákí laced the wine with opium
the companions lost their heads and turbans.

They kept the water of life from Alexander.
It cannot be found with force and gold.

Although reason is the currency of existence,
how can it compare to love, the work of the alchemist?

Come and listen to the state of the anguished ones
who speak with few words and much meaning.

The Chinese idol is the foe of faith and heart.
O lord, guard my heart and faith.

بمستوران مگو اسرار مستی
حـدیث جـان مـپرس از نقش دیوار
بیمن رایت منصور شاهی
عـلم شـد حـافظ انـدر نظـم اشعار
خداوندی بجای بندگان کرد
خداونـدا ز آفـاتش نگهـدار

Don't reveal to the chaste the secrets of drunkenness.
Don't ask the picture on the wall for words of the soul.

Under the illustrious banner of Manṣúr Sháh
Ḥáfiẓ has become skilled in the crafting of verse.

A lord did his duty on behalf of his slaves.
O lord, protect him from calamities.

غزل ۳۸

عیدست و آخر گل و یاران در انتظار
ساقی به روی یار ببین ماه و می بیار
دل برگرفته بودم از ایّام گل ولی
کاری بکرد همّت پاکان روزه دار
دل در جهان مبند و ز مستی سؤال کن
از فیض جام و قصّهٔ جمشید کامکار
جز نقد جان بدست ندارم شراب کو
کان نیز بر کرشمهٔ ساقی کنم نثار
گر فوت شد سحور چه نقصان صبوح هست
از می کنند روزه گشا طالبان یار
ترسم که روز حشر عنان بر عنان رود
تسبیح شیخ و خرقهٔ رند شراب خوار
خوش دولتیست خرّم و خوش خسروی کریم
یارب ز چشم زخم زمانش نگاه دار
می خور بشعر بنده که زیبی دگر دهد
جام مرصّع تو بدین درّ شاهوار
زآنجا که پرده پوشی عفو کریم تست
بر قلب ما ببخش که نقدیست کم عیار
حافظ چو رفت روزه و گل نیز میرود
ناچار باده نوش که از دست رفت کار

Ghazal 38

It's ^{c}*íd*, there is the rose at last, and the friends are waiting. 1
Sákí, see the new moon in my love's face, and bring wine.

My heart had given up on the season of the rose but
the spiritual power of the fast-keepers has accomplished something.

Don't tie your heart to the world, and seek in drunkenness
the cup's bounty and the story of prosperous Jamshid.

My hand holds nothing but the coins of my soul. Where is the wine?
So that I can scatter them, too, after the sákí's glance.

If *ṣabúr* has passed, so what? There is the morning cup. 5
They make seekers of the beloved break their fast with wine.

I fear that on Resurrection Day the shaikh's rosary
and the coat of the wine-drinking rend will be evenly matched.

It is a happy time, we have a kind and generous king.
O God, protect him from the evil eye of time.

Drink wine as you listen to my verse, for your jewelled cup
will give to this royal pearl a different beauty.

To overlook is the essence of your generous forgiveness.
Forgive our heart, which is a coin of few carats.

Ḥáfiẓ, since the fast has gone and the rose will also go, 10
you can only drink wine, it's out of your hands.

غزل ۳۹

ای صبا نکهتی از خاک ره یار بیار
ببر اندوه دل و مژدهٔ دلدار بیار
نکتهٔ روح فزا از دهن یار بگو
نامهٔ خوش خبر از عالم اسرار بیار
تا معطّر کنم از لطف نسیم تو مشام
شمّه‌ای از نفحات نفس یار بیار
بوفای تو که خاک ره آن یار عزیز
بی غباری که پدید آید از اغیار بیار
گردی از رهگذر دوست بکوریّ رقیب
بهر آسایش این دیدهٔ خونبار بیار
خامی و ساده‌دلی شیوهٔ جانبازان نیست
خبری از بر آن دلبر عیّار بیار
شکر آنرا که تو در عشرتی ای مرغ چمن
باسیران قفس مژدهٔ گلزار بیار
کام جان تلخ شد از صبر که کردم بی دوست
عشوه‌ای زآن لب شیرین شکر بار بیار
روزگاریست که دل چهرهٔ مقصود ندید
ساقیا آن قدح آینه کردار بیار
دلق حافظ بچه ارزد بمیش رنگین کن
وآنگهش مست و خراب از سر بازار بیار

Ghazal 39

O dawn wind, bring a whiff of dust from my love's road. 1
Take grief from my heart and bring good news of her.

Repeat for me an uplifting witticism from her mouth.
Bring a letter of good news from the world of secrets.

To perfume my nose, let your gentle breeze
bring a bit of scent from her breath.

On your loyalty, bring dust from that dear love's road,
free of the dust stirred up by strangers.

In spite of my rival, bring dust from her road. 5
With that kohl I can soothe these eyes that rain blood.

Naivete and a simple heart aren't the style of those who give up
their life.
Bring me news of that savvy young thing.

O bird of the field, we rejoice that you live in pleasure.
To the cage's captives bring glad tidings from the rosegarden.

The mouth of my soul grew bitter from waiting without her.
Bring a sultry gesture from those lips that scatter sugar.

For a long time my heart did not see the face it sought.
O Sákí, bring that mirror-like cup.

What's the coat of Ḥáfiẓ worth? Stain it with wine, 10
then bring him, drunk and ruined, from the head of the bazaar.

غزل ۴۰

روی بنما و وجود خودم از یاد ببر
خرمن سوختگانرا همه گو باد ببر
ما چو دادیم دل و دیده بطوفان بلا
گو بیا سیل غم و خانه ز بنیاد ببر
زلف چون عنبر خامش که ببوید هیهات
ای دل خام طمع این سخن از یاد ببر
سینه گو شعلهٔ آتشکدهٔ فارس بکش
دیده گو آب رخ دجلهٔ بغداد ببر
دولت پیر مغان باد که باقی سهلست
دیگری گو بو و نام من از یاد ببر
سعی نابرده درین راه بجائی نرسی
مزد اگر می طلبی طاعت استاد ببر
روز مرگم نفسی وعدهٔ دیدار بده
وانگهم تا بلحد فارغ و آزاد ببر
دوش میگفت بمژگان درازت بکشم
یارب از خاطرش اندیشهٔ بیداد ببر
حافظ اندیشه کن از نازکی خاطر یار
برو از درگهش این ناله و فریاد ببر

Ghazal 40

Show your face and make me forget I exist. 1
And the pile of burned ones, tell the wind to take them.

Since we gave up our heart and eyes to the storm of affliction
say, "Come, flood of sorrow, tear this house from its foundations."

Who can smell his curls, like fresh ambergris?
Alas! O heart, flush with desire, forget this matter.

You could say that my breast overwhelms the fire-temple of Fars.
You could say that my eyes disgrace the Tigris of Baghdad.

Long live the Magus, for the rest is nothing. 5
To anyone else say, "Go, and forget my name."

Make no effort on this road and you will not arrive.
If you seek the reward, do the will of your teacher.

Let me see you for one moment on the day of my death
and then take me, unfettered and free, to my tomb.

Last night he said, "I will kill you with my long eyelashes."
O lord, banish the thought of injustice from his mind.

Ḥáfiẓ, consider the beloved's sensitive nature.
Leave his threshold. Take this whining and wailing with you.

غزل ٤١

گلعذاری ز گلستان جهان ما را بس
در چـــمن سایهٔ آن سرو روان مـــا را بس
من و هم صحبتی اهل ریا دورم باد
از گـــرانان جــهان رطـل گـــران مـــا را بس
قصر فردوس بپاداش عمل میبخشند
مـــا که رندیـــم و گـــدا دیـــر مغان ما را بس
بنشین بر لب جوی و گذر عمر ببین
کـــاین اشارت ز جـــهان گـــذران مـــا را بس
نقد بازار جهان بنگر و آزار جهان
گر شما را نه بس این سود و زیان ما را بس
یار با ماست چه حاجت که زیادت طلبیم
دولت صحبت آن مـــونس جـــان مـــا را بس
از در خویش خدا را ببهشتم مفرست
که سر کوی تو از کون و مکان مـــا را بس
حافظ از مشرب قسمت گله بی انصافیست
طبع چون آب و غزلهای روان مـــا را بس

Ghazal 41

One rose from the world's garden is enough for us. 1
In the field, the shade of that flowing cypress is enough for us.

May I never be intimate with hypocrites.
Of the world's weighty things, a heavy cup is enough for us.

For good deeds they grant you the palace of paradise.
We rends and paupers, the Magi's cloister is enough for us.

Sit by the stream's edge and watch life pass by,
for this sign from a passing world is enough for us.

See the cash in the world's bazaar, and the world's torments. 5
If not enough for you, this profit and loss is enough for us.

The friend is with us. Why would we look further?
Intimacy with that soul-companion is enough for us.

I am here at your door, for God's sake don't send me to heaven,
for in all the universe the head of your alleyway is enough for
us.

Ḥáfiẓ, it is unjust to complain about the wellspring of your fate.
A nature like water and flowing ghazals are enough for us.

غزل ۴۲

دارم از زلف سیاهش گله چندانکه مپرس
که چنان زو شده ام بی سر وسامان که مپرس
کس بامّید وفا ترک دل و دین مکناد
کـه چنانم مـن ازین کرده پشیمان که مپرس
بیکی جرعه که آزار کسش در پی نیست
زحـمتی میکشم از مـردم نـادان کـه مپرس
زاهد از ما بسلامت بگذر کین می لعل
دل و دین می برد از دست بدانسان که مپرس
پارسائی و سلامت هوسم بود ولی
شیـوه ای مـیکند آن نـرگس فتّان کـه مپرس
گفت و گوهاست درین راه که جان بگدازد
هر کسی عربدهٔ این که مبین آن کـه مپرس
گفتم از گوی فلک صورت حالی پرسم
گفت آن میکشم اندر خم چوگان کـه مپرس
گفتمش زلـف بـخون کـه شکستی گفتا
حافظ این قصه درازست بقرآن که مپرس

Ghazal 42

Don't ask me how many complaints I have about her black hair, 1
for I became so undone because of her that it's beyond telling.

Let no one abandon heart and faith in hope of fidelity.
I did this. Don't ask me how sorry I am.

With one innocent drink that hurt no one,
I drew such trouble from the ignorant that it's beyond telling.

Ascetic, pass by. Peace be with you.
Don't ask how this ruby wine destroys heart and faith.

I desired a life of virtue and righteousness but 5
that enticing narcissus is so artful it's beyond telling.

On this road there are disputes that melt the soul.
Each one says loudly, "Don't look at this! Don't ask about that!"

I thought I would ask the orb of heaven how it was with him.
He said, "I suffer so much in the mallet's curve it's beyond
telling."

I said to her, "With whose blood did you curl your hair?"
She said, "Ḥáfiẓ, it's a long story. By the Qur'án, don't ask."

غزل ۴۳

دوش با من گفت پنهان کاردانی تیز هوش
از شما پنهان نشاید کرد سرّ می فروش
گفت آسان گیر بر خود کارها کز روی طبع
سخت می گیرد جهان بر مردمان سخت کوش
وانگهم در داد جامی کز فروغش بر فلک
زهره در رقص آمد و بربط زنان میگفت نوش
با دل خونین لب خندان بیاور همچو جام
نی گرت زخمی رسد آئی چو چنگ اندر خروش
تا نگردی آشنا زین پرده رمزی نشنوی
گوش نامحرم نباشد جای پیغام سروش
گوش کن پند ای پسر وز بهر دنیا غم مخور
گفتمت چون در حدیثی گر توانی داشت گوش
در حریم عشق نتوان زد دم از گفت و شنید
زانکه آنجا جمله اعضا چشم باید بود و گوش
بر بساط نکته دانان خود فروشی شرط نیست
یا سخن دانسته گو ای مرد بخرد یا خموش
ساقیا می ده که رندیهای حافظ فهم کرد
آصف صاحب قران جرم بخش عیب پوش

Ghazal 43

Last night a wise, keen-minded one whispered to me, 1
"The wine-seller's secret should not be hidden from you.

He said, 'Take it easy, for by its nature
the world is hard on those who try hard.'

And then he gave me a cup, and in its light, across the heavens,
Venus began to dance, and played her lute, and cried, 'Drink!'

While your heart bleeds let your lips smile like the cup.
Don't, if you are struck, break into a roar like the harp.

Until you are an initiate you will not hear a secret in this music. 5
The outsider's ear is no place for the angel's message.

Listen to my advice, O son, and don't worry about the world.
I told you a pearl-like *ḥadíth* if you can hear it.

In love's sanctuary there is no murmur of debate
because there all your limbs must be eye and ear.

In the shop of those who understand subtlety, hawking oneself
is not allowed. Speak knowingly, O wise one, or be quiet."

O Sákí, give us wine, because Áṣaf of auspicious birth,
forgiver of sins and overlooker of faults, understands what Ḥáfiẓ
 really means.

غزل ٤٤

فاش میگویم و از گفتهٔ خود دلشادم
بندهٔ عشقم و از هر دو جهان آزادم
طایر گلشن قدسم چه دهم شرح فراق
که درین دامگه حادثه چون افتادم
من ملک بودم و فردوس برین جایم بود
آدم آورد درین دیر خراب آبادم
سایهٔ طوبی و دلجوئی حور و لب حوض
بهوای سر کوی تو برفت از یادم
نیست بر لوح دلم جز الف قامت دوست
چکنم حرف دگر یاد نداد استادم
کوکب بخت مرا هیچ منجّم نشناخت
یارب از مادر گیتی بچه طالع زادم
تا شدم حلقه بگوش در میخانهٔ عشق
هردم آید غمی از نو بمبارکبادم
میخورد خون دلم مردمک دیده سزاست
که چرا دل بجگر گوشهٔ مردم دادم
پاک کن چهرهٔ حافظ بسر زلف ز اشک
ورنه این سیل دمادم ببرد بنیادم

Ghazal 44

I speak frankly and that makes me happy: 1
I am the slave of love, I am free of both worlds.

I am a bird from heaven's garden. How do I describe that separation,
my fall into this snare of accidents?

I was an angel and highest paradise was my place.
Adam brought me to this monastery in the city of ruin.

The houris' caress, the pool and shade trees of paradise
were forgotten in the breeze from your alleyway.

There is nothing on the tablet of my heart but my love's tall *alif*. 5
What can I do? My master taught no other letter.

No astrologer knew the constellations of my fate.
O lord, when I was born of mother earth which stars were rising?

Ever since I became a slave at the door of love's tavern
sorrows come to me each moment with congratulations.

The pupil of my eye drains the blood from my heart.
I deserve it. Why did I give my heart to the darling of others?

Wipe the tears from Ḥáfiẓ's face with soft curls
or else this endless torrent will uproot me.

غزل ٤٥

خرّم آن روز کزین منزل ویران بروم
راحت جان طلبم وز پی جانان بروم
گرچه دانم که بجائی نبرد راه غریب
من ببوی سر آن زلف پریشان بروم
چون صبا با دل بیمار و تن بی‌طاقت
بهواداری آن سرو خرامان بروم
دلم از وحشت زندان سکندر بگرفت
رخت بر بندم و تا ملک سلیمان بروم
در ره او چو قلم گر بسرم باید رفت
با دل زخم‌کش و دیدهٔ گریان بروم
نذر کردم گر ازین غم بدر آیم روزی
تا در میکده شادان و غزلخوان بروم
بهواداری او ذرّه صفت رقص‌کنان
تا لب چشمهٔ خورشید درخشان بروم
تازیان را غم احوال گرانباران نیست
پارسایان مددی تا خوش و آسان بروم
ور چو حافظ نبرم ره ز بیابان بیرون
همره کوکبهٔ آصف دوران بروم

Ghazal 45

Happy that day that I leave this ruined house. 1
I seek rest for my soul. I will go after the beloved.

Although I know that the stranger's road leads nowhere,
I will follow the scent of his touseled curls.

Even with sick heart and failing body, like the dawn wind
I will go to adore that striding cypress.

My heart grew weary in the isolation of Alexander's prison.
I will pack my things. I will go to the kingdom of Solomon.

Even if I must travel his road on my head, like a pen, 5
I will go with a weeping eye and a wounded heart.

I vowed that if I emerge from this sorrow one day
I will go merrily to the tavern door, singing ghazals,

and adoring him, like a dust mote, dancing,
I will go to the edge of the sun's blazing source.

Nimble riders don't feel the pain of the heavily-burdened.
Saintly ones, help me go with ease and happiness.

And if, like Ḥáfiẓ, I don't find my way out of the wilderness,
I will travel in the train of Áṣaf of the ages.

غزل ٤٦

فتوی پیر مغان دارم و عهدیست قدیم
که حرامست می آنجا که نه یارست ندیم
چاک خواهم زدن این دلق ریائی چکنم
روح را صحبت نـا جنس عـذابیست الیم
تا مگر جرعه فشاند لب جانان بر من
سالهـا شـد کـه منم بـر در میخانه مقیم
مگرش خدمت دیرین من از یاد برفت
ای نسیـم سحـری یـاد دهش عهـد قدیم
بعد صد سال اگر بر سر خاکم گذری
سر بـر آرد ز گلـم رقص‌کنان عظم رمیم
دلبر از ما بصد امّید ستد اوّل دل
ظاهراً عهـد فرامش نکنـد خلـق کـریـم
غنچه گو تنگدل از کار فرو بسته مباش
کـز دم صبح مـدد یـابی و انفاس نسیـم
فکر بهبود خود ای دل ز دری دیگر کن
درد عـاشق نشود بـه بمـداوای حکیـم
گوهر معرفت اندوز که با خود ببری
کـه نصیب دگـرانست نصـاب زر و سیم
دام سخت است مگر یار شود لطف خدا
ورنه آدم نـبرد صـرفه ز شیطـان رجیـم
حافظ ار سیم و زرت نیست چه شد شاکر باش
چـه به از دولـت لطـف سخـن و طبع سلیـم

Ghazal 46

I have the judgment of the Magus and it is an ancient promise:
"Wine is forbidden unless your love is your companion."

I want to tear this coat of hypocrisy. What can I do?
Intimacy with unworthy people is torture to the soul.

On the chance that her lip might sprinkle me with wine
I have lived for years in the tavern doorway.

Has she forgotten my ancient service? O wind of dawn,
Remind her of those days, and of her promise.

If, in a hundred years, you pass by my grave,
my rotted bones will rise up from the mud, dancing.

At first she stole our heart with a hundred hopes.
Usually generous people do not forget a promise.

Say to the rosebud, "Don't despair that you are tightly folded,
for the dawn wind's breath will bring you life."

O heart, ponder your health at another doorway.
The lover's sickness will not improve in a physician's care.

Gather up the jewels of gnosis to carry it with you,
for wealth in gold and silver is the lot of others.

The snare is strong unless God's grace befriends you.
Otherwise what advantage did Adam have over Satan?

Ḥáfiẓ, you lack silver and gold. So what? Be thankful.
What can surpass the blessings of sound nature and exquisite
verse?

غزل ۴۷

وصال او ز عمر جاودان به
خـداوندا مـرا آن ده کـه آن به
بشمشیرم زد و با کس نگفتم
که راز دوست از دشمن نهان به
شبی میگفت چشم کس ندیدست
ز مـرواريد گـوشم در جهان به
خدارا از طبیب من بپرسید
کـه آخر کی شود این ناتوان به
بخلدم دعوت ای زاهد مفرمای
که این سیب زنخ زان بوستان به
دلا دایم گدای کوی او باش
بحکـم آن که دولت جـاودان به
بداغ بندگی مردن بدین در
بجـان او کـه از ملک جهان به
جوانا سر متاب از پند پیران
کـه رای پیر از بخت جـوان به
گلی کان پای‌مال سرو ما گشت
بـود خـاکش ز خون ارغوان به
سخن اندر دهان دوست گوهر
ولیکن گفتهٔ حافظ از آن بـه

Ghazal 47

Union with him is better than eternal life.
O lord, give me that which is better.

He struck me with his sword and I told no one.
My love's secret is better hidden from the enemy.

One night he said, "No one has seen in the world
anything better than the pearl of my ear."

For God's sake, ask my physician,
"When will this feeble one finally get better?"

O ascetic, don't summon me to heaven,
for the apple of his chin is better than that orchard.

O heart, be forever a beggar in his alleyway, for, as they say,
it's better to have wealth that is everlasting.

By his soul, it is better to die a slave on this threshold
than to rule the world.

O youth, don't shun the advice of your elders,
for the master's judgment is better than beginner's luck.

The dust of a rose trampled by our cypress
is prettier than the blood of the redbud tree.

In the mouth of the beloved speech is a jewel.
However, the verse of Ḥáfiẓ is better than that.

غزل ۴۸

دوش رفتم بدر میکده خواب آلوده
خرقه تر دامن و سجاده شراب آلوده
آمد افسوس کنان مغبچهٔ باده فروش
گفت بیدار شو ای رهرو خواب آلوده
شست و شوئی کن و آنگه بخرابات خرام
تـا نگردد ز تو این دیر خراب آلوده
بهوای لب شیرین پسران چند کنی
جـوهـر روح بیاقـوت مـذاب آلـوده
بطهارت گذران منزل پیریّ و مکن
خلعت شیب چو تشریف شباب آلوده
آشنایان ره عشق درین بحر عمیق
غــرقه گشتند و نگشتند بآب آلوده
پاک و صافی شو و از چاه طبیعت بدر آی
کــه صفائی نــدهد آب تراب آلوده
گفتم ای جان جهان دفتر گل عیبی نیست
گر شود فصل بهار از می ناب آلوده
گفت حافظ لغز و نکته بیاران مفروش
آه ازین لطـف بـانـــواع عتاب آلـوده

Ghazal 48

Last night I went to the tavern door stained with sleep,
my cloak-hem soaked, my prayer mat stained with wine.

The wineseller's Magian boy came and shook his head
and said, "Wake up, traveller, you are stained with sleep!

Wash yourself, and then stride into the tavern,
so you won't stain this cloister with ruin.

In your desire for young boys' lips for how long
will you sully the pearl of your spirit with melted ruby?

Remain pure in the waystation of old age,
and don't stain the mantle of age as you did the trappings of
youth.

In this deep sea, those who know love's road
were drowned and never touched by water.

Come forth pure and clear from the well of your nature,
for muddy water will not make you clean."

I said, "O soul of the world, what can be wrong
if in springtime the book of the rose is stained with pure wine?"

He said, "Ḥáfiẓ, don't peddle wisecracks and witticisms to the
friends."
Ah, for this kindness, stained with many kinds of reproach!

غزل ۴۹

این خرقه که من دارم در رهن شراب اولی
وین دفتر بی معنی غرق می ناب اولی
چون عمر تبه کردم چندانک نگه کردم
در کنج خراباتی افتاده خراب اولی
چون مصلحت اندیشی دورست ز درویشی
هم سینه پر از آتش هم دیده پر آب اولی
من حالت زاهد را با خلق نخواهم گفت
کین قصّه اگر گویم با چنگ و رباب اولی
تا بی سر و پا باشد اوضاع فلک زین دست
در سر هوس ساقی در دست شراب اولی
از همچو تو دلداری دل بر نکنم آری
چون تاب کشم باری ز آن زلف بتاب اولی
چون پیر شدی حافظ از میکده بیرون آی
رندی و هوسناکی در عهد شباب اولی

Ghazal 49

This cloak I have is better pawned for wine, 1
and this meaningless notebook is better drowned in it.

Now that I look back at my wasted life,
it is better to have fallen down drunk in the tavern corner.

Prudence and proper thoughts lie far from the dervish way.
Better to fill your breast with fire and your eye with tears.

I will tell no one about the ascetic's indiscretions.
To tell this story I need rabab and harp.

As long as the heavens remain so insolent, 5
it's better to have your mind on the sákí and your hand on the
wine.

No, I will never let go of a love like you.
Since I must burn, better that it be because of your curly hair.

You have grown old, Ḥáfiẓ, so come out of the tavern.
Revelry and the rend's life are better suited to the days of youth.

غزل ۵۰

ای بیخبر بکوش که صاحب خبر شوی
تـــا راه‌رو نباشـــی کـــی راهبـــر شـــوی
در مکتب حقایق پیش ادیب عشق
هـــان ای پســـر بکوش کـــه روزی پدر شوی
دست از مس وجود چو مردان ره بشوی
تـــا کیمیای عشـــق بیابـــیّ و زر شـــوی
خواب و خورت ز مرتبهٔ خویش دور کرد
آنگه رسی بخویش که بی خواب و خور شوی
گر نور عشق حق بدل و جانت اوفتد
بالله کـــز آفتـــاب فلـــک خـــوبتر شـــوی
یکدم غریق بحر خدا شو گمان مبر
کـــز آب هـــفت بحـــر بیـــک موی تر شوی
از پای تا سرت همه نور خدا شود
در راه ذوالـجـلال چـــو بـــی پـــا و سر شوی
وجه خدا اگر شودت منظر نظر
زیـــن پس شکی نمانـــد که صاحب نظر شوی
بنیاد هستی تو چو زیر و زبر شود
در دل مدار هیچ چو زیر و زبر شوی
گر در سرت هوای وصالست حافظا
باید که خاک درگه اهل نظر شوی

Ghazal 50

O ignorant one, try to become a master of knowledge.
If you are not a traveler how can you become a guide?

In the school of truth listen carefully to the tutor of love
so that one day, O son, you can become a father.

Like those worthy of the path, wash your hands of the copper of existence
so that you can find the philosopher's stone of love, and become gold.

Sleeping and eating have kept you far from your station.
You will arrive at your self when you give up sleeping and eating.

If the light of the love of truth falls on your heart and soul,
by God, you will become lovelier than the sun in heaven.

For a moment drown yourself in the sea of God and don't believe
that the seven seas will wet a single hair.

From head to toe you will become the light of God
when you lose yourself on His glorious road.

Once God's face becomes the object of your sight
there is no doubt that you will become a master of vision.

When the foundations of your existence become topsy-turvy,
have nothing in your heart, for you will also become topsy-turvy.

O Ḥáfiẓ, if desire for union fills your head
you must become dust in the doorway of those who see.

NOTES

These notes are numbered according to the *bayt* to which the annotation refers.

GHAZAL 1

Meter: o--- o--- o--- o---
Hazaj muthamman sálim

This is the opening *ghazal* of Háfiz's *Díwán*. It draws on much of the imagery found in classical Arabic *qaṣídas*, in which the poet remembers the beloved who has left her campsite, and whom he seeks forever after in the desert wilderness. For an introduction to the *qaṣída* form, and some beautiful translations, see Sells, *Desert Tracings*.

The first and last *miṣra'* of this ghazal are in Arabic. Tradition says that the opening line was taken from the poetical works of the Umayyad caliph Yazíd ibn Mu'áwiya (d. 683), conqueror of eastern Iran and murderer of Imam Husayn.

Once again, the reader must bear in mind that Persian pronouns do not indicate or express gender. In *bayts* 4 and 7 the translation could indicate a masculine beloved (see Translator's Introduction, p. 8 and notes).

Bayt

1 *sáqí.* The cupbearer, usually a young man, beautiful and adored, who brings the wine of love to those in the tavern (see Translator's Introduction p. 10); also the elusive friend or beloved, a Magian boy (see below, note to *bayt* 3), a beautiful and distracting idol (see notes to Ghazal 12).

2 *náfeh,* the musk-bag of the graceful gazelle (the beloved), the scent of which draws and guides the lover in his search through the desert.

3 *pír-i mughán,* the Elder or Master of the Magi, who were Zoroastrian fire-worshippers and thus, in Islamic terms, unbelievers. Unconstrained by the Islamic prohibition against alcohol, Zoroastrians or Mazdeans (and Christians) operated taverns, and the Magus is the tavern-master, the source of wine (with all its heretical and spiritually symbolic associations).

The Magus is also a *pír* or *shaykh,* a spiritual master, who guides his disciples along the states and stations of the spiritual path (see notes to Ghazal 4), with which he is intimately familiar. His guidance and instructions must be followed absolutely, even if they appear outwardly to be in contravention of religious law.

Literal translation of the second *miṣra'*: "for such a traveller is not ignorant of the road and its stopping-places/stations."

4 Here and elsewhere the first person plural may refer to the community of lovers, or to the lover and his beloved, or to Ḥáfiẓ alone.

The impermanence of the caravanserai suggests the world in which we live, and seek to find pleasure.

6 The mystics' secret is the joy of union with God, and this is what is spoken of, or recollected (see *dhikr*, notes to Ghazal 20), in mystic assemblies. Such a joyous secret is hard to keep. The error of the great mystic Ḥalláj was to reveal this secret (see notes to Ghazal 24).

7 Literal translation of the first *miṣra'*: "If you desire (his/her) presence/attention, never be absent/fall into oblivion, Ḥáfiẓ."

ghá'ib and *ḥuḍúr*, "absence" and "presence," two opposites, are states encountered on the mystical path; if one seeks the presence of God, one must be absent from oneself. (See Schimmel, *Mystical Dimensions of Islam*, p. 129 and ff. for additional discussion of such paired states.)

GHAZAL 2
Meter: o-o- oo— o-o- oo-
Mujtaththth makhbún maḥdhúf
Bayt

2 *rind*, rend (see Darush Shayegan's Introduction, "The Visionary Topography of Ḥáfiẓ," pp. 28 ff. and Translator's Introduction p. 9).

rabáb, a stringed instrument use to accompany a lyric or song.

3 *khirqa*, a patched frock or coat, usually of dark blue wool, which a *pír* bestows upon one who has performed preliminary service and now formally enters upon the mystical path. See the notes to Ghazal 4 for a discussion of Ḥáfiẓ's view of *khirqa*-wearing Sufis and other followers of the mystical path.

deyr-i mughán, the monastery of the Magi, the tavern (see notes to Ghazal 1).

6 *síb-i zanakhdán*, literally the "apple of the chin," which often has a dimple (*cháh*, literally "well") in the center of it; a source of beauty, and hence distraction, to the lover. Ḥáfiẓ often uses these images and words for delightful, and usually untranslatable, wordplay.

7 *kuḥl*, kohl, the black powder placed around the eyes of children and others, thought to help one see better.

8 *ṣabr*, one of the stations of the mystical path, is patience in the face of affliction, patience to accept God's will in whatever form it comes. *Ṣubúrí*, an advanced form of *ṣabr*, is patience under any and all circumstances.

GHAZAL 3
Meter: o-o- oo— o-o- —
Mujtathth makhbún aslam
Bayt

1 *ṣabá*, the wind of dawn, traditionally comes from the east, and is auspicious. It brings news of, or scent from, the beloved; it opens rose buds; and it relays the lover's love to his beloved.

For more on the lover pursuing the gazelle of his beloved, see introductory note to Ghazal 1.

2 Parrots were considered intelligent because of their facility with speech, and were thought to love sugar because their talk is so sweet. "Sugar-eating parrot" may describe a good poet, and in this *bayt* describes the lover, seeking sugar from his beloved.

4 The rose and nightingale are a classic pair in Persian, Turkish, and other Islamic poetry. The nightingale, as lover, always seeking love from the source of eternal beauty, its beloved, the rose.

6 The moon, like the rose and nightingale, is a classic image in Persian poetry, suggesting the face of the Beloved (which is pure beauty), that with which one desires the utmost intimacy.

8 *samá'*, literally "song" or "hearing," has come to mean the ritual, usually collective, singing of *ghazals* or other mystical verses. It is also the concert and ecstatic dance practiced by some Sufi orders and condemned by the more austere and orthodox. The dance of the "Whirling Dervishes" of the Mevlevi order in Konya, Turkey, is the example of this form of *samá'* most familiar to occidentals.

zuhra, the planet Venus, heaven's musician, see note to Ghazal 21.

masíḥ, Jesus, the Messiah, one of the major prophets of Islam. The breath of the *masíḥ* is the breath of life, and can raise the dead, as Jesus did Lazarus (see note to Ghazals 18 and 24).

GHAZAL 4
Meter: —o -o-o o—o -o-
Muḍári' akhrab makfúf maḥdhúf

Bayt

1, 2 As a rule, "Sufi" in Ḥáfiẓ's *Díwán*, does not carry a positive connotation. While Ḥáfiẓ usually uses *'árif* and *darwísh* to describe true seekers of the mystical path, by the late fourteenth century many viewed the structured Sufi orders, *ṭaríqahs*, to be worldly organizations operating beneath a veneer of spirituality, and thus corruptions of the original ideals of mystical brotherhood. In this and the following *bayt* he strikes a contrast between the *rend* (a true seeker of the way) and the Sufi and *záhid*, ascetic, who wear only the external trappings of piety.

In Ḥáfiẓ, *bíya*, literally "come," also carries the sense of "look here," "bring," "agree with me that," "meditate on the fact that."

2 *ḥál* (pl. *aḥwál*), state. The mystical path has both states and stations (*maqám*, pl. *maqámát*). A disciple, through his (or her) own striving and with appropriate guidance, reaches different stations (or stages, "stopping-places") as he proceeds along the path. States come to, and depart from, the disciple's heart by God's will, independent of the disciple's efforts. Some of these states and stations are described in later notes, and a comprehensive discussion of the path and its states and stations can be found in Schimmel, *Mystical Dimensions*, pp. 98 and ff.

3 The *'anqá*, or *símurgh*, is a mythical bird, known by name but not by sight, that lives on Mt. Qáf, the mountain that encircles the world. The Simurgh is the symbol of the Divine Presence or Essence of God, of Truth, in *Manṭiq aṭ-ṭayr*, "The Birds' Conversation," by classical Persian poet Faríd ud-Dín 'Aṭṭar (d. 1220).

4 Adam, the first man and an emblem for mankind, was persuaded by Satan to eat of

the Tree of Eternity in Eden. As a result, God forced him to leave the garden and its cool water sources (Suras 20:120 and 2:30).

8 *muríd*, a novice or disciple that has chosen to follow the mystical path under the guidance of a *pír* (see notes to Ghazal 1).

ṣabá, dawn wind, see notes to Ghazal 3.

Jám is located in the large province of Khurasan, now in eastern Iran near the Afghan border. The Shaykh of Jám to whom Ḥáfiẓ refers is probably Shaykh al-Islám Aḥmad Námiqi Jámí, known as Shaykh Zhindih Pil (1063-1141). The shaykh was strict and severe in his preaching against, and condemnation of the drinking of wine. Hence the irony of Ḥáfiẓ's closing *miṣra'*.

GHAZAL 5
Meter: —o -o-o o—o -o-
Muḍári' akhrab makfúf maḥdhúf

Bayt

1 Wine has a rich array of meanings and resonances in Persian poetry, and is associated with light, illumination, and truth. The tilted wineglass can suggest sunrise to the drinker, the sun itself takes light from the wine.

2 The surface of the wine in the wine cup reveals the face of the Beloved, the reflection of one's own face (which is a mirror of God, as His creation, and therefore is Him), and, if the cup is Jamshid's (see note, Ghazal 16), can reveal the world itself.

3 The *sarw* or cypress tree is an image of the tall, graceful, elegant stature of the beloved. The *ṣanawbar* or fir tree is used in the same way, but less frequently.

5 Literal translation: "I fear that on the Day of Resurrection the (religiously) lawful bread of the *shaykh* will carry no more advantage than our (religiously) forbidden water (= wine)."

6 The initial *miṣra'* can be read two ways: (1) "To the eye of our witness-to-beauty (i.e. the beloved) drunkenness is good/pleasing" or (2) "the drunkenness that comes (to me) because of/from the eye of the witness-to-beauty is good."

7 The Friends are flowers in the garden.

10 Probably Qavám ud-Dín Hasan (d. 1353), vizier to Abú Isḥáq Injú, one of Ḥáfiẓ's early patrons.

GHAZAL 6
Meter: -o— oo— oo— oo-/—
Ramal sálim makhbún maḥdhúf

Bayt

1 *saḥar* means first light, not the moment of sunrise.

'ayyár (pl. *'ayyárán*) has no exact equivalent in English. It can describe someone who is is nimble and intelligent, who moves quickly here and there, who is something of a vagabond and sometimes a bandit, trickster, or charlatan. The *'ayyárán* were also a *futuwwah*, a mens' club similar to an order of chevaliers.

2 *wádí-yi ayman*, (*íman*, "safe, secure") according to tradition, the riverbed in Sinai where God called to Moses (Suras 20:12 and 79:16).

3 In the second *miṣra'* the word that Ḥáfiẓ uses for tavern is *kharábát* (literally "house of ruin"), playing off the word "ruin" (*kharáb*) in the first *miṣra'*.

4 *ishárát*, signs, omens, or allusions to mystical truths.

6 Insane people were often chained. Here the word for chains, *silsilah*, carries with it the sense of linkages: lover to beloved, successions of *pírs* in a given *ṭaríqa*, a strong rope of tradition extending back to the Qur'án and to God.

GHAZAL 7
Meter: —o -o-o o—o -o-
Muḍárí akhrab makfúf maḥdhúf

Bayt

4 *karím*, the Generous, one of the attributes and names of God.

5 Here the garments and clothes suggest the physical body, in contrast to the soul.

8 To sustain himself, the lover needs a life-giving kiss from the beloved.

9,10 *mudda'í*, the false lover, or impostor, does not understand true love, has not suffered its pain, and composes his verse for self-advancement. See Translator's Introduction, p. 9, and Meisami, *Medieval Persian Court Poetry*, p. 268, 296.]

GHAZAL 8
Meter: o-o- oo— o-o- oo-/—
Mujtathth makhbún maqṣúr

Bayt

2 *himma*, "high spiritual energy or ambition," spiritual power that enables an adept to attain higher planes of experience and understanding, and that enables the *pír* to protect his disciples.

3 *surúsh*, the angel of inspiration, messenger and guide to poets, sometimes synonymous with Gabriel. Here *surúsh* is the voice that is the contact, the aural connection, with the invisible world.

4 *sidra-nishín*, one who sits in the *sidra*, one of the trees of Paradise that provide shade to those who hold God's throne.

sháhbáz, royal falcon. This is often an image for man, God's favorite falcon, who longs be called home, just as a hunting falcon is called back to the prince's wrist with a drum.

6 *pír-i ṭaríqat*, master of the *ṭaríqat*, the spiritual path or roadway traveled by the disciple, that branches off from the wider thoroughfare of Islamic law (*sharí'a*). Schimmel, *Mystical Dimensions*, p. 98.

8 *gham-i jahán khurdan*, literally "to drink the sorrow/suffering of the world."

GHAZAL 9

Meter: o-o- oo— o-o- oo-/—
Mujtathth makhbún maqṣúr

Bayt

1 *khálí az khalal*, "empty of/without flaw or impurity," meaning without the type of flaw that one finds in a precious stone, or the type of impurity that one finds in a wine.

safína, literally "boat," meant in Ḥáfiẓ's time a small book with narrow pages that contained selected verse, and could be carried in one's sleeve or in the folds of one's turban.

2 *'áfíyat*, literally "health," but here in the spiritual sense, i.e. salvation.

3 Literal translation: "I am not the only one in the world who is afflicted from lack of practice, the affliction of the *'ulema* is also from knowledge/learning without practice." That is, they have knowledge, but do nothing with it.

6 The curls, or tresses, are chains that bind, but that also link one to God. See also notes to Ghazal 6.

zuhra, Venus, is considered an auspicious planet, see notes to Ghazals 3 and 21. *zuḥl*, Saturn, the black planet, is considered highly inauspicious.

7 *azal*, "pre-eternity," the period before Creation, before God's primordial covenant with man. See Shayegan, "The Visionary Topography of Ḥáfiẓ," pp. 19-22.

GHAZAL 10

Meter: -o— oo— oo— oo-/—
Ramal sálim makhbún maḥdhúf

Bayt

2 *nargis*, the narcissus, hangs its head and suggests the languid, sultry, or perhaps intoxicated eyes of the beloved. It is often used to mean simply "eyes."

3 *derína*, "ancient," does not refer to the age of the poet, but means "of old," from a long time ago.

4 *'árif*, a mystic, disciple, a true seeker of God. See also notes to Ghazal 4.

5 *záhid*, ascetic. See notes to Ghazal 4.

rúz-i alast, the "Day of Alast" was the time of God's primordial covenant with man (Sura 7:171), see Shayegan, "The Visionary Topography of Ḥáfiẓ," p. 21.

7 *tauba*, a vow of repentance that must be serious and eternal in order to be acknowledged and accepted by God; also the name of the initial station of the mystical path, in which one repents and turns away from the snare that is the world in order to seek a higher reality.

GHAZAL 11

Meter: -o— oo— oo— oo-/—
Ramal sálim makhbún maḥdhúf

Bayt

2 *ṭilismat,* talismans, here can also mean magic formulae or spells.

3 Literal translation of first *miṣra'*: "The palace of Paradise, to which Riḍwán went to be its doorkeeper. . ." Riḍwán is the gatekeeper of Heaven.

4 *qalb-i siyáh,* "black heart," also means "fool's gold."

ṣuḥbat, "society, friendship, conversation" also means intense intimacy, whether between lover and beloved or between a *pír* and his disciple.

7 *qibla,* the direction of prayer; in Islam, the Ka'ba in Mecca toward which all Muslims direct the recital of their canonical prayers, and with which all mosques are aligned.

9 *az azal tá bi-abad,* "from before pre-Eternity/Creation until eternity-without-end." See Shayegan's, Introduction, pp. 19-22.

10 *himma,* spiritual power; see notes to Ghazal 8.

11 Qárún, like Croesus, had treasures "such that the very keys of them were too heavy a burden for a company of men endowed with strength." (Sura 28:76) Qárún exulted in his wealth, believing that his own wisdom, and not God's will, was the source of his good fortune. God had the earth swallow Qárún beneath the weight of his possessions.

For a discussion of *gheyrat,* here translated as "wrath," see notes to Ghazal 15.

13 Áṣaf ibn Barkhíya, vizier to Solomon, was viewed as a wise and model statesman. Here the reference probably refers to one of two of Háfiz's patrons, both referred to elsewhere as Áṣaf Tháni: Qavám ud-Dín Muḥammad Ṣáḥib-i 'Ayar, or Khwajah Jalál ud-Dín Tauranshláh, both viziers to Sháh Shujá'.

GHAZAL 12

Meter: -o— oo— oo— oo-/—
Ramal sálim makhbún maḥdhúf

Bayt

1 *but,* (pl. *bután*) idol, carries with it most of its English connotations (including the religious condemnation of idolaters as unbelievers), but usually refers to the beloved, or to a person of great, and thus distracting, sensual beauty.

2 A "soul-seeing eye" is one capable of seeing the truth, of seeing into the essential nature of things. In the second *miṣra'* Ḥáfiẓ laments that his eye, distracted by worldly things, has not yet reached this stage or level of development.

5 *faqr,* poverty, the quality of being unattached to material things, is a source of spiritual wealth, and a central aim and concern to those setting out on, and travelling along, the mystical path.

6 In the second *miṣra'* Ḥáfiẓ uses the word *sulṭán,* which means "king," creating a nice contrast to the constable in the first *miṣra'*. In this context *sulṭán* can also mean God.

7 The Ka'ba (see also notes to Ghazal 11) is the shrine of black stone in the Great Mosque at Mecca. It is the endpoint of the great pilgrimage of the Ḥajj.

8 Khusrau Parvíz was the last great Sassanian king, whose story was well-known from Firdawsi's epic *Sháhnámeh.* His love for the Armenian Christian princess Shirin is the topic of Niẓámí's *Khusrau and Shírín. Khusraushírín* also means "sweet king," creating wordplay in the final *bayt* and probably referring to a patron, who is now listening to Ḥáfiẓ's stories of love.

GHAZAL 13
Meter: —o -o-o o—o -o-
Muḍári' akhrab makfúf maḥdhúf
Bayt

3 Literal translation of the second *miṣra'*: "Be the consoler of yourself/your own pain-drinker. What is the pain of time/fate?" (i.e. do not fret about, or be distracted by, the world).

4 *Iram*, a city in Yemen where a legendary garden was built by the Arab king Shaddad to duplicate Paradise. It was destroyed by a storm sent as a warning against such hubris (Suras 89:6-8 and 34:16). This may also be a reference to a specific garden in Shiraz.

7 Kawthar is one of the fountains or ponds of Paradise.

GHAZAL 14
Meter: —o -o-o o—o -o-
Muḍári' akhrab makfúf maḥdhúf
Bayt

1 *ján sipárdan*, "to entrust one's soul," also means "to become devoted or initiated" or "to give up one's life."

2 *istikhárah*, divination or prognostication, usually to ascertain whether something is auspicious or inauspicious by letting a Qur'án fall open and reading the page, or by taking a random segment of prayer beads and counting them out. The *Díwán-i Ḥáfiẓ* is also used for divination in this manner.

3 According to a *ḥadíth qudsí*, a tradition or saying which has come directly from God but which is not found in the Qur'án, God said, "I was a hidden treasure, and I loved to be known, so I created the world." See Shayegan, "The Visionary Topography of Ḥáfiẓ,", p. 19.

4 The *shaḥnih*, watchman, constable, or policeman, i.e. Reason, has no jurisdiction in this *wiláyat.* The *shaḥnih* also appears in Ghazal 12, *bayt* 6.

wiláyat, "province, dominion, territory" can also mean "saintship, holiness, sanctity," a quality possessed by accomplished mystics.

5 *máh párih*, the beautiful one, literally means "sliver/piece of moon."

6 In Persian short vowels are not written. Depending on whether the short vowel

here is "i" or "u," the verb here can mean either "pulling" (*kishad*) or "killing" (*kushad*), and is meant to suggest both.

GHAZAL 15

Meter: -o— oo— oo— oo-/—
Ramal salim makhbun mahdhuf

Bayt

1 *kawn-o makán*, literally "existence/creation" and "place/locality," denotes the created universe, physical reality.

3 The *sidra* (see notes to Ghazal 8) and the *ṭúbá* are tall shade trees in Paradise.

6 *faná'*, meaning death or annihilation, is also a technical term in the mystical lexicon. In such a context *faná'*, "annihilation," describes the mystic's goal: it is the reverse of coming-into-being or becoming, being the (re)absorption of the mystic into the Divine Essence. This is not a union of two separate entities, but a return to man's pre-Creation state, when he was in God. The moth when it burns upon being joined to the candle flame it seeks, experiences *faná'*.

7 *gheyrat*, an almost untranslateable term that has no equivalent in English, meaning sometimes "jealousy or possessivenes," "zeal," "wrath," "ardor," "intense energy or enthusiasm." Here, Ḥáfiẓ cautions the *záhid* (see notes to Ghazal 4) not to become too complacent or smug in his charade of zealousness, as God can tell the difference between false and true spiritual zeal.

In the second *miṣra'* Ḥáfiẓ contrasts the ascetic's cloister with the *deyr-i mughán*, the monastery of the Magi (the tavern). See also notes to Ghazal 1.

GHAZAL 16

Meter: —o -o-o o—o -o-
Muḍári' akhrab makfúf maḥdhúf

The imagery throughout this ghazal intertwines the act of loving with the act of making the *ḥajj*, or pilgrimage to the Sacred Enclosure and Ka'ba at Mecca.

Bayt

3 *bakht*. In English, "luck" usually carries only a positive connotation. In Persian it means luck of any sort, good or bad, and thus is similar to, although less weighty than, "fate" or "destiny."

5 *muḥtasib*, the equivalent of a religious constable or policeman, who makes his rounds of the city to ensure that the provisions of the *sharí'a* (such as those against drinking alcohol) are being obeyed.

Jamshid, one of the first mythical kings of Persia, is found in the *Sháhnámeh* of Firdausi. He possessed a goblet which revealed the entire world to the person looking into it. Iram (see notes to Ghazal 13) was said to be his seat of power, and his cup was of no help in averting the garden city's destruction by God.

6 *ḥarím-i ḥaram*, "sacred enclosure/sanctuary," refers usually to the precincts of Mecca and Medina. It can also be understood as proximity to the Beloved.

7 *bibar guy*, a term drawn from the game of polo, means to "take/steal the ball" and take it down the field to victory.

mudda'í, see notes to Ghazal 7.

GHAZAL 17
Meter: -o— oo— oo— oo-
Ramal sálim makhbún maḥdhúf

Bayt

2 *bigardash narasídím*, literally "we did not reach her/his dust," meaning that as the Beloved took off, no matter what we did, we couldn't even reach the dust stirred up by her/him and slowly settling on the road s/he took.

3 *fátiḥa*, the opening Sura of the Qur'án; *ḥirz yamání*, an auspicious prayer which Muḥammad supposedly learned from Uways Qaraní, an illiterate, on the road to Yemen; *ikhláṣ*, Sura 112 of the Qur'án. The first two of these prayers are part of the *namáz*, the Muslim's ritual prayer, and all are normally addressed to God and to God alone. Despite the recital of these prayers, said in order to to prevent the Beloved from departing, s/he left.

GHAZAL 18
Meter: —o -o-o o—o -o-
Muḍári' akhrab makfúf maḥdhúf

Bayt

2 When a candle begins to sputter, its wick is trimmed with a knife or scissors, after which it burns again with a bright and steady flame.

Literal translation of the second *miṣra'*: "and this old man (literally "man-who-has-eaten-the-years") began youth (again) from the beginning."

4 *pistih*, a pistachio, conveys the image of the mouth: tiny, partly opened lips, smiling.

5 *'ísádam*, one who has the breath of the Messiah, Jesus. An *'ísádam* can breathe life into inanimate objects, heal the sick, and raise the dead (Sura 5:109), as the beloved can do for the lover. See also notes to Ghazal 3.

7 Literal translation: "Because of this talk/story the seven domes of Heaven are full of clamor. See the short-sighted one who took the tale/talk/verse to be of little importance."

8 *ta'wídh*, an amulet, usually consisting of verses from the Qur'án tightly rolled and encased in metal and worn on the person. Verses concerning the *'ísádam* are considered exceptionally auspicious.

GHAZAL 19
Meter: -o— oo— oo— oo-
Ramal sálim makhbún maḥdhúf

This *ghazal* is discussed in detail by Meisami in *Medieval Persian Court Poetry*, pp. 286-297, "The Analogical Structure of a Persian Courtly Lyric" and "The World's Pleasance."

Bayt

3 The pearls and rubies that the tip of the eyelash(es) must pierce are the tears and heart-blood that flow from the eyes of the lover.

4 *abad*, eternity-without-end, see notes to Ghazal 11.

5 The rosegarden of Iram, see notes to Ghazal 13.

6 Jamshid, see notes to Ghazal 16. The "throne of Jamshid" to which Ḥáfiẓ speaks may refer also to his patron Abú Isḥáq, a patron, whose passing Ḥáfiẓ laments here.

A literal translation of the second *miṣra'*: "It said, Alas, for that waking (i.e. good) fortune/realm has gone to sleep."

8 *ṣabr*, patience, see notes to Ghazal 2.

GHAZAL 20
Meter: —o -o-o o—o -o-
Muḍári' akhrab makfúf maḥdhúf

Bayt

1 The wise hoopoe (*hudhud*) was a friend to King Solomon who could understand the language of birds. It was the hoopoe that first brought Solomon news of the Queen of Sheba (Sura 27:20). In Persian poetry the hoopoe is a go-between, the bird that leads the lover to the beloved. In 'Aṭṭár's *Manṭiq uṭ-ṭayr* it was the hoopoe who led the other birds in quest of the *símurgh* (see notes to Ghazal 4).

3 *qurb*, "proximity," is one of the stages of the mystical path. It has been explained by 'Alí ibn 'Uthmán al-Hujwírí as "an ethical proximity, brought forth by the fulfillment of God's orders, the opposite of separation from God, caused by man's disobedience." (Cited from *Kashf al-Mahjúb*, Schimmel, *Mystical Dimnesions*, p. 133.)

In the first *miṣra'* Ḥáfiẓ says that there is no station that is simultaneously near (to the beloved or to God) and far (from the beloved or from God). In the second *miṣra'* he says that he can see "you" clearly (implying proximity) but sends off a prayer to "you" (implying distance).

4 The east wind and north wind, respectively the winds of morning and evening, are trusted carriers of prayers, messages, and scents. See also notes to Ghazal 3.

8 *qawl*, a short lyric poem or saying, which, like the *ghazal*, is often sung.

10 *dhikr* is the Sufi practice of "recollecting" or "remembering" God. This recollection and constant repetition of God's names (or other formulae deemed appropriate by the *pír* or *shaykh*) takes many forms, and can be performed silently or aloud, alone or in the company of fellow dervishes, sometimes with music. Like other forms of silent prayer or collective meditiation in other religions, *dhikr* is considered a primary tool in developing the adept's spiritual concentration and assisting his or her progress.

GHAZAL 21
Meter: —o -o-o o—o -o-
Muḍári' akhrab makfúf maḥdhúf

Bayt

2 Supplicants touch or clasp the hem of the person of whom they are asking assistance.

3 The *miḥráb* is the arched prayer-niche in a wall, aligned with the Ka'ba in Mecca, toward which one prays.

4 Literal translation: "If I must go the way of Hárút of Babylon . . ." Hárút and Marút of Babylon (Sura 2:101) were two angels, capable of great magic, whom God sent to earth. A woman, Venus (*zuhra*), was impressed with their magical powers and tricked them into telling her God's greatest name, which she then used to turn herself into a star. God, in his anger, hung the two sorcerer angels upside down in a well near Babylon, where they are always thirsty but can never reach the water.

GHAZAL 22
Meter: -o— -o— -o-
Ramal maḥdhúf

Bayt

5 The Zindehrúd is the river that flows through the city of Isfahan, north of Shiraz.

GHAZAL 23
Meter: o— o— o— o—
Hazaj muthamman sálim

Bayt

1 *kháṭirí*, "a heart/mind" that is *majmú'*. *Majmú'* is a technical term used by mystics to mean spiritually-focused, not distracted by material or worldly things.

2 Literal translation of the second *miṣra'*: "the one who kisses that threshold must have his life/soul in his sleeve (from whence he can scatter it, as he must, like coins)."

3 According to the Qur'án Solomon had an inscribed seal which gave him power over animals and spirits.

4 *khaṭṭ*, means both a line of written script and also the line of new down moustache that appears on the upper lip of the beloved, a sensuous boy on the edge of manhood.

Because the Persian script does not distinguish among short vowels, the *khaṭṭ* of the beloved can be read as either "dark" (*mishkin*) or "musk-scented" (*mushkin*).

6 *faqír-i rah-nishín*, "road-sitting pauper." A true *faqír* is one whose life is lived in complete accord with the quality of *faqr* (see notes to Ghazal 12).

8 Legendary kings Kay Khusrau (see notes to Ghazal 12) and Jamshid (see notes to Ghazal 16).

GHAZAL 24
Meter: oo—/-o— oo— oo— oo-/—
Ramal sálim makhbún maḥdhúf

Bayt

1 Jamshid's cup, see notes to Ghazal 16.

2 The "shell of the *kawn-o makán*," the universe, see notes to Ghazal 15.

3 The *pír-i mughán*, the master of the Magi. See notes to Ghazal 1.

While *dúsh* means literally "last night," it can also refer to *azal*, pre-eternity or the eve of creation (see notes to Ghazal 9).

4 The mirror here suggests both the surface of the world-seeing cup and the heart of the Magus himself, as the mystic's task is to constantly polish his or her heart so that it may better reflect God and his manifestations.

5 *ḥakím*, "the Wise," is one of the names or attributes of God.

The blue dome is the arch of the heavens.

6 *sar-i dár boland gashtan*, means both "to raise up (erect)" and "to raise up (ennoble)" the gallows.

This *bayt* refers to Ḥusayn ibn Manṣúr al-Ḥalláj (857-922), the famous Sufi martyr who came to symbolize the ecstasy, as well as the suffering, of the lover's personal union with God. His fault, according to the Sufi tradition, was that he openly revealed his great secret to the ears of the uninitiated by declaring to the populace of Baghdad, "*áná'l-ḥaqq*," "I am the Truth (one of the Names of God)," the ultimate expression of complete undifferentiated union with God. For this heresy against orthodox interests, and for political reasons, he was sentenced to death during the reign of al-Muqtadir, and was, after a lengthy imprisonment, hung and beheaded. He is said to have danced all the way to the gallows.

7 *aḥwál*, "states" (*ḥál*, sing.). Although the word is most often used in the ordinary sense of "state, condition," *ḥál* is also technical term in Islamic mysticism. See notes to Ghazal 4.

8 Literal translation of the *bayt*: "All these sleights-of-hand tricks that he, i.e. reason, was doing here, the sorcerer was doing before the rod and white hand (of Moses)."

Pharaoh called upon Moses to prove that he was indeed a messenger from God by staging a competition between Moses and Pharaoh's own sorcerers. Moses cast down his rod, which turned into a serpent. He then drew his hand forth from his robes and it glowed with a white light. In the face of these miracles Pharoah's sorcerers withdrew from the competition (Sura 7:104 ff.).

9 Literal translation of the second *miṣra'*: "others will also do that which the messiah was doing (i.e. breathing life into inanimate or dead things)." See *'ísádam*, notes to Ghazal 18.

10 The dark chains of the idol's (beloved's) hair are both the cause of, and the relief for, Ḥáfiẓ's love-frenzied heart. The idol, *but*, is discussed in the notes to Ghazal 12.

GHAZAL 25

Meter: o-o- oo— o-o- —
Mujtathth makhbún aṣlam

Bayt

1 Jamshid, see notes to Ghazal 16.

kuḥl, kohl, see notes to Ghazal 2.

3 The dawn wind serves the rose, the object of its desire, and in response the rose drops the green of its outer bud and blossoms. The lover serves his beloved in this way, as does the disciple his master.

7 *ṭabi'at*, "nature," meaning the natural functions or temper of man.

ṭaríqat, the spiritual path, see notes to Ghazal 8.

8 The sputtering candle, see notes to Ghazal 18.

10 *ḥaqíqat*, "truth" or "reality," here in the sense of ultimate spiritual reality.

GHAZAL 26

Meter: -o—/oo— oo— oo— oo-/—
Ramal sálim makhbún maḥdhúf

One of the most cryptic of Ḥáfiẓ's *ghazals*, this is considered by many who follow the mystical path to be the finest of them. The discussions of this *ghazal* in the various commentaries are lengthy, explore in detail the various levels of meaning, and are not replicated here.

Bayt

1 *azal*, see notes to Ghazal 9.

tajallí, "manifestation," "revelation," "illumination," making-visible.

The relationship between God and creatures can be condensed, very roughly, in this way: "The Absolute yearned in His Loneliness, and according to the tradition, "I was a hidden treasure and I wanted to be known, so I created the world," produced creation as a mirror for His *tajallíyát*, His manifestations." Schimmel, *Mystical Dimensions of Islam*, p. 268. See Shayegan, "The Visionary Topography of Ḥáfiẓ," pp. 18-19.

2 *gheyrat* has no English equivalent, and blends the qualities of jealousy, possessiveness, anger, intense energy, and zeal. See also notes to Ghazal 15.

On the Day of Alast (see notes to Ghazal 10) God first offered the burden of His love to the heavens with its angels and heavenly host, to the earth, and to the mountains. They were fearful, and refused to accept it. Adam made the foolish choice to accept it. This trust (*amánat*) defines mankind's special relationship to God. (Sura 33:72) See Shayegan, "The Visionary Topography of Ḥáfiẓ," pp. 25-26 and also Ghazal 29.

3 Reason, the enemy of love, seeks to acquire some of love's light. Love will not allow it.

gheyrat, see above, *bayt* 2.

4 The impostor (*mudda'í*, see notes to Ghazal 7) also wants access to the secret of love, but as he is not an intimate (*maḥram*, consanguine) love sends him packing.

6 *ján 'ulwí*, the "celestial or angelic soul" (as opposed to one of the lower souls).

GHAZAL 27

Meter: o-o- oo— o-o- —

Mujtathth makhbún aṣlam

Bayt

4 *nargis*, the eyes as a narcissus, see notes to Ghazal 10.

5 Literal translation of the second *miṣra'*: "where is the lion-hearted one who does not/will not avoid calamity/affliction?"

6 *ṣabúrí*, patience, see notes to Ghazal 2.

GHAZAL 28

Meter: -o— oo— oo— oo-/—

Ramal sálim makhbún maḥdhúf

Bayt

3,4 See notes to Ghazal 4 for a discussion of the way in which Sufis, wearers of the *khirqa* (see notes to Ghazal 2), are viewed by Ḥáfiẓ. Ḥáfiẓ distinguishes here between true mystics and those who only wear the external trappings of mystics.

4 "Our story" can mean either (a) the story that Ḥáfiẓ tells about his love or (b) the story that others tell about Ḥáfiẓ and his outrageous behaviors.

6 *azal tá bi-abad*, see notes to Ghazal 11.

8 *nargis*, the narcissus, is discussed in notes to Ghazal 10. The phrase *chashm-i bímár*, the sultry and languid eyes of the beloved, means literally "sick eyes." That the narcissus tried to mimic the beloved's "sick eyes," sets up wordplay between the two *miṣra'*.

9 Hearts and souls were thought to nest in the beloved's hair. See also Ghazal 30.

GHAZAL 29

Meter: -o-- oo— oo— oo-/—

Ramal sálim makhbún maḥdhúf

Bayt

1 Adam was made from clay kneaded and formed with love by God's own hand, and then given life by God's breath. The angels were commanded by God to bow down to Adam, because unlike the angelic host, part of man's nature is divine (that is, love). (Sura 15:29)

paymánih, "cup," creates a nice visual pun, as in Persian *paymán* means "treaty" or "covenant," linking to *bayt* 3.

3 *amánát*, see notes to Ghazal 26.

4 These are the seventy-two sects of Islam.

ḥaqíqat: truth, ultimate reality (see also notes to Ghazal 25).

6 According to the Qur'án, the downfall of Adam and Eve was by means of a cereal grain, not a piece of fruit.

GHAZAL 30

Meter: o— o— o— o—

Hazaj muthamman sálim

Bayt

2 The second *miṣra'* can be read as either to "scatter" or "sacrifice" the souls of lovers, which were thought to nest, like birds, in the beloved's hair.

3 *kháṭir* means both "heart" and "mind." See also notes to Ghazal 23.

7 The martyr Ḥusayn ibn Manṣúr al-Ḥalláj, see notes to Ghazal 24.

GHAZAL 31

Meter: -o— -o— -o— -o-

Ramal maḥdhúf

Bayt

1 *vá'iz*, the preacher who leads communal prayer in the mosque.

The *miḥráb* is the niche toward which Muslims pray during communal prayer; the *minbar* is the pulpit from which a preacher speaks to those assembled in the mosque.

2 *tauba*, repentance, see notes to Ghazal 10.

3 *dávar*, "the Judge," is one of the names or attributes of God.

4 *bí niyází*, "needlessness" is considered by some to be a station on the mystical path.

6 Adam was created out of clay, but, unlike the angels, was also created out of God's love, thus his dual nature. See notes to Ghazal 29.

8 *khánaqah*, the physical building(s) that house Sufi activities and personnel.

10 Much medieval teaching was done by rote, and the clamor of schoolchildren trying to memorize sections of the Qur'án or other types of verse can still be heard rattling through the streets in parts of the Islamic world.

GHAZAL 32

Meter: oo—/-o— oo— oo— oo-/—

Ramal sálim makhbún maḥdhúf

Bayt

1, 3 *daftar*, a notebook in which one wrote poems or other things. One could also read this as an image for the poet's heart or soul.

3 In medieval times one often washed the ink writing from a notebook when what was written was no longer needed in order to re-use the notebook.

4 In the first *miṣra'*, *án* means a quality that is difficult to express, "a certain or special something."

bután, idols, see notes to Ghazal 12.

dar 'ilm-i naẓar can mean (a) in the "science of the gaze," (see Shayegan, "The Visionary Topography of Ḥáfiẓ," pp. 29-30) (b) in the science of crafting intricate and sophisticated verse, or (c) in the science of the study of the *sharí'a* or religious law; Ḥáfiẓ doubtless wants us to savor the irony of all three meanings.

5 A compass (*pargár*, in the first *miṣra'*) has two legs: the one that is fixed (*pá*, "foot") and the one that moves (*sar*, "head"). In the second *miṣra'* Ḥáfiẓ plays nicely on this in his use of "bewildered" (*sar-gashteh*, "head-turned") and "firm" (*pá bar já*, "foot in place").

8 Mystics traditionally wore coats of blue wool.

Rose-colored suggests that Ḥáfiẓ is referring to the wine master of the tavern.

GHAZAL 33
Meter: oo—/-o— oo— oo— oo-/—
Ramal sálim makhbún maḥdhúf
Bayt

2 Slaves wore in their ear a ring which indicated both their slave-status and the identity of their master.

3 *himmat*, spiritual ambition or power, see notes to Ghazal 8.

5 Young men from various Turkic tribes were thought to be most beautiful, and were prestigious slaves (see text of Ghazal 31, *bayt* 5).

GHAZAL 34
Meter: -o— oo— oo— oo-/—
Ramal sálim makhbún maḥdhúf
Bayt

3 Jamshid, see notes to Ghazal 16.

The seal of Jamshid may be lips of the beloved; the image of God or the beloved falls on the ruby bezel of the lover's heart.

GHAZAL 35
Meter: —o -o——o -o—
Muḍári' akhrab sálim
Bayt

1 *agar bar áyad* can mean both "if it comes to pass" and "if it comes up over the horizon."

3 *khayál*, the dream image or phantom image of the beloved that comes at night, or in one's sleep.

GHAZAL 36
Meter: o-o- oo— o-o- oo-/—
Mujtathth makhbún aṣlam
Bayt

4 Parrots love sugar, see notes to Ghazal 3.

GHAZAL 37
Meter: o— o— o—
Hazaj maqṣúr

Bayt

2 The literal translation of the phrase "may you live long" is "may your head be green," word play on the color of the parrot.

3, 6 *ḥarífán* can mean either "companions" or "rivals."

4 A literal translation of the phrase "bright luck" is "awake (good) luck." On luck generally, see notes to Ghazal 16.

To waken a sleeper, one sprinkles rosewater on their face. Rosewater "from the cup" can here be a reference to wine, which wakes one from unawareness and ignorance.

5 *dar pardah* here can mean that the minstrel played his melody (a) "on the fret (of his instrument)," (b) "within/behind the veil," and/or (c) "within a certain (musical) mode."

7 According to the legends and romances of the time, Alexander the Great of Macedon spent his life wandering the world in search of the water of life. While both Alexander and his guide Khiḍr (see below) arrived at the well or fountain, Khiḍr was granted the ability to actually find the water, and drank it, becoming immortal. Alexander was not granted that reward.

Khiḍr, a mysterious servant of God in the Qur'án, was a companion and teacher of Moses (Sura 18:65). Although invisible, Khiḍr is often present to assist, to teach, or to initiate a disciple, and is an important figure in Islamic mystic circles.

10 Representational art was forbidden by Islamic law because it distracted the faithful and tempted them into idolatry. Of all representational art, Chinese paintings and portraits were considered the most beautiful and intricate, and therefore the most dangerous.

11 While beautiful and distracting, paintings and images are lifeless, and have no divine essence.

12-13 These are probably references to Abú Isḥáq, one of Ḥáfiẓ's patrons, but can also suggest a reference to Ḥalláj (see notes to Ghazal 24).

GHAZAL 38
Meter: —o -o-o o—o -o-
Muḍari akhrab makfúf maḥdhúf

Bayt

1 Among critics and commentators there is debate as to the meaning of the first *miṣra'* of this *ghazal.* Some believe that it means that the arrival of the festival of the lesser *'íd* (that marks the beginning of the lunar month of Shawwál and the end of Ramaḍán, the month of fasting) coincides with the withering of the last rose. Other read it as meaning that the arrival of *'íd* means that once again the rose, with its brief life, can be the focus of attention. It is the latter meaning that has been chosen here.

The end of Ramaḍán is signaled by the arrival of the new moon. The fast is decreed to be over when the slightest sliver of new moon becomes visible to the religious authorities.

In the Persian tradition, what one sees directly after their first look at a new moon is of tremendous importance, and should be auspicious. One should gaze at a new moon, and then try to have one's eyes fall directly on the object of one's desire, perhaps one's beloved, or something of similar beauty. Here, in the second *miṣra'*, one can read the beloved's face as being a/the new moon, or one can read the *miṣra'* as instructing the sákí to look at the wine or the friend's face after looking at the moon, or to look from the friend's face to the wine (and what is reflected in it).

2 The *himmat*, spiritual power or ambition (see notes to Ghazal 8), of those who kept the fast has accomplished something: bringing the fast to an end so that one can get back to wine and roses.

3 Jamshid, see notes to Ghazal 16.

5 *saḥúr* is the (usually large) meal eaten just before first light, to fortify oneself for the upcoming day-long fast. The fast goes from first light until sunset.

It is unclear as to whether this line means that (a) at sunset, lovers break the day of fasting with wine (which, of course, is prohibited by Islamic law under any circumstances) or whether (b) given that *saḥúr* has passed, lovers break the laws of fasting completely and drink wine during the day.

9 *pardah púshí*, to cover discreetly from the eyes of others; to overlook is one of God's attributes.

GHAZAL 39
Meter: oo—/-o— oo— oo— oo-/—
Ramal sálim makhbún maḥdhúf
Bayt

5 *kuḥl*, kohl, see notes to Ghazal 2.

6 *'ayyár*, translated here as "savvy," has a variety of meanings difficult to capture in English. See notes to Ghazal 6.

9 The cup of wine reflects one's own face, and that face is a creation of God's and therefore is the essence of God, and God is the ultimate beloved. See also notes to Ghazal 24, *bayt* 4.

GHAZAL 40
Meter: -o— oo— oo— oo-
Ramal sálim makhbún maḥdhúf
Bayt

1 This bayt suggests the state of *faná'*, "annihilation," see notes to Ghazal 15.

4 Ḥáfiẓ's heart burns with such intensity that it overwhelms and extinguishes the fires

of the major Zoroastrian fire temple in southern Iran. His eyes cry such tears that the river Tigris is embarrassed.

5 *pír-i mughán*, see notes to Ghazal 1.

GHAZAL 41

Meter: -o— oo— oo— oo-/—
Ramal sálim makhbún maḥdhúf

Bayt

3 *deyr-i mughán*, see notes to Ghazal 2.

4 *ishárat*, see notes to Ghazal 6.

7 *kawn-o makán*, see notes to Ghazal 15.

GHAZAL 42

Meter: -o— oo— oo— oo-/—
Ramal sálim makhbún maḥdhúf

Bayt

5 *nargis*, the narcissus, see notes to Ghazal 10.

7 Ḥáfiẓ assumes that the great orb of heaven would not be subject to the afflictions described in the preceding *bayts*. Upon inquiring, he learns that even the orb of heaven suffers the same blows, pain, and abrupt changes in direction that the ball receives from the curved mallet in a game of polo. Polo was a popular courtly sport, and the mallet was sometimes used as an image for the beloved's curls, in which the lover's head was caught.

GHAZAL 43

Meter: -o— -o— -o— -o-
Ramal maḥdhúf

Bayt

2 "He" refers to the wine-seller, and this *bayt* reports the wine-seller's secret, as heard by the keen-minded one of *bayt* 1.

3 *zuhrah*, Venus, see notes to Ghazal 21.

4 *zakhmí rasídan* means both "to be struck/receive a blow/wound" as a person and "to be struck" as a string in a musical instrument.

5 "You will not hear a secret *zín pardah*," meaning both "from this fret/mode, i.e. in this music or melody" and "within/(from) inside the veil." See notes to Ghazal 37.

6 Generally, *ḥadíth* means a saying, maxim, or piece of advice. It may have that meaning here, and refer to the *bayt*'s advice to "not worry about the world." *Ḥadíth* also can mean a divine saying or story of God or the Prophet. If read in this sense, it may refer to the paraphrase in *bayt* 7 of a famous *ḥadíth qudsí* (a divine revelation that is not contained in the Qur'án).

7 This *bayt* paraphrases and refers to a *ḥadíth qudsí* which describes a form of the

station of *qurb*, "proximity" (see notes to Ghazal 20). *Qurb* is achieved by performing more than the ordinary acts of devotion. Schimmel quotes God's words from Abu Naṣr as-Sarráj: "My servant ceases not to draw nigh unto me by works of devotion, until I love him, and when I love him I am the eye by which he sees and the ear by which he hears" (*Mystical Dimensions*, p. 133).

8 Literally *basáṭ* means "on the blanket," as in medieval times (and in villages today) vendors display their wares on blankets.

9 A literal translation of the first *miṣra*ʿ: "O sákí, give wine, for he (Áṣaf, identified in the second *miṣra*ʿ) understood the *rend*-like behaviors and actions of Ḥáfiẓ."

Áṣaf, see notes to Ghazal 11.

GHAZAL 44
Meter: oo—/-o— oo— oo— oo-
Ramal sálim makhbún maḥdhúf

Bayt

1 The poet is free of attachment, hence free of both this world and the next.

2 The "snare place of the phenomenal world," in contrast to heaven's garden.

4 *ṭúbá*, see notes to Ghazal 15.

Kawthar, see notes to Ghazal 13.

The second *miṣra*ʿ means both "with the breeze/air of the head of your alleyway" and "with desire/longing for the head of your alleyway."

5 *lawḥ* means both the tablet or slate on which one writes and the tablet of a tombstone.

alif, the first letter of the Persian and Arabic alphabets, and in the name Alláh. It also serves as the numeral "1" (its numerical value in Islamic numerology), and to all Muslim mystics signifies the oneness and unity of God. It also suggests that tall and willowly figure of the beloved.

8 In the first *miṣra*ʿ Ḥáfiẓ explains that his eyes have grown red from crying, and that the red tears he sheds now are draining the blood from his heart.

GHAZAL 45
Meter: oo—/-o— oo— oo— oo-/—
Ramal sálim makhbún maḥdhúf

Bayt

2 The poet understands that as long as he is not one of the beloved's intimates, he will wander aimlessly and never reach his goal. Nevertheless, he chooses to follow the beloved's scent.

4 *waḥshat*, a stage in the mystical path that is characterized by a "feeling of loneliness, of being far from intimacy, lost in the wilderness." See Schimmel, *Mystical Dimensions*, p. 132.

The prison of Alexander (said to be in Isfahan, and not related to Alexander the Great) serves as an image of the confines of this earthly life, in contrast to the kingdom of Solomon, an image of heaven.

5 The untranslateable pun in the second *miṣra‘* plays with the pen image in the first: the "torn or wounded heart" means also the split quill that forms the point of the pen, and the "crying eye" means the small well at the head of the quill's split that holds the ink after the pen is dipped in ink.

8 *tázíyán*, those who travel quickly and lightly, on horseback, also means Arabs, or Arab horses. *pársáyán*, those who are saintly or abstemious, can also mean Persians.

9 Áṣaf, see notes to Ghazal 11.

GHAZAL 46
Meter: oo—/-o— oo— oo— oo-/—
Ramal sálim makhbún maḥdhúf

Bayt

1 *fatwá*, the sentence or judgment issued by a religious judge.

9 *ma‘rifa*, "gnosis," intuitive or divinely inspired (as opposed to a rational) understanding of God, is one of the highest stations of the mystical path. An *‘árif* is a mystic who has reached this advanced station (see notes to Ghazal 4).

10 Adam is often, as here, a symbol for all mankind.

GHAZAL 47
Meter: o— o— o—
Hazaj maḥdhúf

Bayt

5 *síb-i zanakh*, the "apple of the chin," see notes to Ghazal 2.

8 *pír* (and its plural, *pírán*) can mean simply "elder" or "old one," or refer to a spiritual master (see notes to Ghazal 1), or, as here, imply both.

9 *arghawán*, the redbud or Judas-tree, whose deep red blossoms look like the heartblood of lovers.

GHAZAL 48
Meter: oo—/-o— oo— oo— oo-/—
Ramal sálim makhbún maḥdhúf

Much of the imagery here refers to or suggests the ritual ablutions required by the *sharí‘a*. One must perform ablutions before entering a mosque, after relieving oneself, after menstruation, or after sexual or other unclean activity.

Bayt

1 *dúsh*, see notes to Ghazal 24.

GHAZAL 49
Meter: --o o--- --o o---
Hazaj akhrab sálim

Bayt

4 The *záhid*'s behavior has been inconsistent with his outwardly pious demeanor, and consistent with the contents of a sensuous song.

rubáb, see note to Ghazal 2.

5 *bí sar-o pá* can mean "insolent, mean, nasty," in the manner of a "low-life" or "punk"; and also means "without beginning or end."

6 In the second *miṣra'*, *táb* is used twice, playing on its meanings of "a twist or curl" and "a glow or burning."

GHAZAL 50
Meter: —o o-o- o—o -o-
Muḍári' akhrab makfúf maḥdhúf

Bayt

2 The second *miṣra'* can also be read to say "for one day you will become a father."

3 *wujúd*, "existence," usually refers to the existence of God into which the mystic is dissolved at the stage of *faná'* (see notes to Ghazal 15). Here it suggests earthly existence, or attachment to the material world.

7 Literal translation of the second *miṣra'*: "when on the road of the possessor-of-glory (a name or attribute of God) you lose head and foot."

9 *zír-o zabar*, literally "under and over," refers to the "overturning of hearts" that will occur at the Resurrection. One whose heart is free of attachment to the world is already in a state of union with God, and will be unaffected.

SELECTED BIBLIOGRAPHY

Andrews, Walter G. *Poetry's Voice, Society's Song: Ottoman Lyric Poetry.* Seattle and London: University of Washington Press, 1985.

Arberry, A. J. "The Art of Háfiz." In *Aspects of Islamic Civilization as Depicted in the Original Texts.* London: George Allen & Unwin, 1964: 344-58

——. "Háfiz and His English Translators." *Islamic Culture,* 20 (1946): 111-128 and 229-49.

——. "Orient Pearls at Random Strung." *Bulletin of the School of Oriental and African Studies* 11 (1943-1946): 699-712.

——. "Three Persian Poems." *Iran,* 2 (1964): 1-12.

Bausani, Alessandro. "Ghazal." *Encyclopedia of Islam (New Edition),* B. Lewis, V. L. Menage et al., ed. London: Luzac and Co., 1971.

Boyce, Mary. "A Novel Interpretation of Ḥáfiẓ." *Bulletin of the School of Oriental and African Studies* 15 (1953): 279-88.

Browne, Edward G. *A Literary History of Persia,* 4 vols. Cambridge: The University Press, 1920. Reprinted, 1969.

Chittick, William C. *The Sufi Path of Knowledge.* Albany: SUNY Press, 1989.

——. *The Sufi Path of Love.* Albany: SUNY Press, 1985.

Ḥáfiẓ-i Shírází, Shams ud-Dín Muḥammad (d. 1389):

Díwán-i Shams ud-Dín Muḥammad Ḥáfiẓ-i Shírází. Edited by N. Ahmad and S. M. R. J. Nai'ini. Tehran: Amir Kabir, 1971.

Díwán-i Khwajah Ḥáfiẓ-i Shírází. Edited by A. Anjaví Shirazi. Second edition. Tehran: 'Elmi, 1967.

Díwán-i Ḥáfiẓ Edited by P. N. Khanlarí. Tehran: Khwarezmí, 1980.

Díwán-i Ḥáfiẓ. Edited by H. Pizhman. Tehran: Beroukhim, 1939.

Díwán-i Shams ud-Dín Muḥammad Ḥáfiẓ-i Shírází, M. Qazvíní and Q. Ghání, eds. Tehran: Zavvar, 1941.

Hillman, Michael. "Ḥáfiẓ and Poetic Unity through Verse Rhythms." *Journal of Near Eastern Studies* 31 (1972): 1-10.

——. *Iranian Culture: A Persianist View.* Lanham: University Press of America, 1990.

——. "Sound and Sense in a *Ghazal* of Ḥáfiẓ." *The Muslim World* 61.2 (1971): 112-21

——. *Unity in the Ghazals of Ḥáfiẓ.* Studies in Middle Eastern Literatures, No. 6. Minneapolis and Chiacgo: Bibiliotheca Islamica, 1976.

Hodgson, Marshall G. S. *The Venture of Islam*, 3 vols. Chicago and London: University of Chicago Press, 1974.

Khurramsháhí, Bahá'al Dín. *Ḥáfiẓ-Námeh.* Tehran: Surush, 1987.

——. *Dhihn wa Zaban-i Ḥáfiẓ.* Tehran, 1982, 1989.

Meisami, Julie Scott. "Allegorical Gardens in the Persian Poetic Tradition." *International Journal of Middle East Studies* 17 (1985): 229-60.

——. "Allegorical Techniques in the Ghazals of Ḥáfiẓ." *Edebiyat* 4.1 (1979): 1-40.

——. "The Analogical Structure of a Persian Courtly Lyric: Háfiz's 81st Ghazal." Paper presented at the Nineteenth International Congress on Medieval Studies, Kalamazoo, Michigan, May, 1984.

——. *Medieval Persian Court Poetry.* Princeton: Princeton University Press, 1986.

——. "The World's Pleasance: Háfiz's Allegorical Gardens." *Comparative Criticism* 5 (1983): 153-85.

——. "Norms and Conventions of the Classical Persian Lyric: A Comparative Approach to the Ghazal." *Proceedings of the 9th Congress of the International Comparative Literature Association.* Innsbruck, 1979, vol. 1.

——. "Sir William Jones and the Reception of Persian Literature." *South Asian Review* 8.5 (1984): 61-70.

Pursglove, Parvin. "Translations of Háfiz and Their Influence on English Poetry since 1771: A Study and Critical Bibliography." Ph. D. Thesis, University College of Swansea, Wales, 1983.

Rajá'í, Aḥmad 'Alí. *Farhang-i Ash'ár-i Ḥáfiẓ*, Vol. 1. Tehran: Zavvar, 1961.

Rehder, Robert M. "The Text of Ḥáfiẓ." *Journal of the American Oriental Society* 94 (1974): 145-56.

——. "New Material for the Text of Ḥáfiẓ." *Iran* 3 (1965).

——. "The Unity of the Ghazals of Ḥáfiẓ." *Der Islam* 51 (1974): 55-96.

Rypka, Jan, and others. *History of Iranian Literature.* Jahn, Karl ed. Dordecht, Holland: D. Reidel, 1968.

Schimmel, Annemarie. *As Through a Veil: Mystical Poetry in Islam.* New York: Columbia University Press, 1982.

——. "Háfiz and His Critics." *Studies in Islam* 16 (1979): 1-33.

——. *Mystical Dimensions of Islam.* Chapel Hill: University of North Carolina Press, 1975.

——. "Persian Poetical Symbolism." Mimeographed. Cambridge: Harvard University, 1979.

——. *A Two-Colored Brocade: The Imagery of Persian Poetry.* Chapel Hill and London: The University of North Carolina Press, 1992.

Schroeder, Eric. "Verse Translation and Ḥáfiẓ." *Journal of Near Eastern Studies* 7 (1947): 209-222.

——. "The Wild Deer Mathnawí." *Journal of Aesthetics and Art Criticism* 11 (1952): 118-34.

Sells, Michael A., transl. *Desert Tracings: Six Classic Arabian Odes by 'Alqama, Shanfara, Labid, 'Antara, Al-A'sha, and Dhu al-Rumma.* Middletown: Wesleyan University Press, 1989.

Stetkevych, Suzanne, ed. *Reorientations: Studies in Arabic and Persian Poetics.* Bloomington: Indiana University Press, 1993.

Súdi Busnaví (d. 1591). *Sharḥ-i Súdí bar Ḥáfiẓ.* Translated by 'Esmat Sattarzadeh. 3rd printing, 4 vols. Tehran: Rangin, 1969.

Wickens, G. M. "An Analysis of Primary and Secondary Significations in the Third Ghazal of Ḥáfiẓ." *Bulletin of the School of Oriental and African Studies* 14 (1952): 627-38.

——. "Ḥáfiẓ." *Encyclopedia of Islam (New Edition)*, 1971.

——. "The Persian Conception of Artistic Unity and Its Implications in Other fields." *Bulletin of the School of Oriental and African Studies* 14 (1952): 239-43.

Yarshater, Ehsan. "The Theme of Wine Drinking and the Concept of the Beloved in Early Persian Poetry." *Studia Islamica* 13 (1960): 43-53.

——. "Persian Poetry in the Timurid and Safavid Periods." *The Cambridge History of Iran*, vol. 6. Cambridge: The University Press, 1986.

Yousofi, Gholam Hosein. "Colors in the Poetry of Ḥáfiẓ." *Edebiyat* 2.2 (1977): 15-28.

SELECTED TRANSLATIONS

Arberry, A. J. *Fifty Poems of Háfiz.* Cambridge: The University Press, 1947.

Avery, Peter and Heath-Stubbs, John. *Thirty Poems.* London: Murray, 1952.

Bell, Gertrude. *Poems from the Dáván of Háfiz.* London: W. Heinemann, 1928.

Bicknell, Herman. *Háfiz of Shiraz.* London: Trubner and Co., 1875.

Boylan, Michael. *Hafez: Dance of Life.* Washington, D. C.: Mage, 1988.

Clarke, H. Wilberforce. *The Divan-i Háfiz.* Cambridge: The University Press, 1891. Reprinted, New York: Samuel Weiser, Inc., 1970.

Cloutier, David. *News of Love: Poems of Separation and Unions by Háfiz of Shiraz.* Greensboro: Unicorn Press, 1984.

Jones, Sir William. *A Grammar of the Persian Language.* London: Parbury, Allen and Co., 1828.

Leaf, Walter. *Versions from Háfiz.* London: G. Richards, 1898.

La Galienne, Richard. *Odes from the Divan of Háfiz.* London: Duckworth and Co., 1905.

Nott, John. *Select Odes from the Persian Poet Hafez.* London: T. Cadell, 1787.

Payne, John. *The Poems of Shemseddin Mohammed Háfiz of Shiraz.* London: Villon Society, privately published, 1901.

Persia Society of London. *Selections from the Rubaiyat and Odes of Háfiz.* London: J. M. Watkins, 1920.